Back
IN THE
Day

"These recipes were my favorites growing up because they were good and I enjoyed the taste and textures. After being exposed to all kinds of foods around the world, these still are my favorites. My mom would make these types of dishes from scratch and with a lot of love. I miss her."

—DK Kodama
Chef and Restaurateur

"Timeless recipes for cooks of all ages. Lynette shares her collection of her mother's treasury of retro recipes in this cookbook which features some of her family favorites.

You'll find just the right recipes for any occasion and you're sure to add new variations to old favorites. So, stir up your 'back in the day' kitchen memories and cook up some fun."

—Muriel Miura, CFCS
*Author of more than 30 Hawai'i cookbooks
and national television cooking show host*

"Lynette has always gathered people of different backgrounds together with her delicious passion for cooking and heartfelt hospitality. This cookbook is a collection of amazing recipes so that you too can enjoy and have fun with your family and friends."

—Regino Ojano III
*Former Pastry Chef
for Pig & The Lady and Piggy Smalls*

"It's the universal peace maker: food. It brings us together, it comforts us. I always look forward to Lynette's cooking! She has once again come up with 'ono recipes! Looking forward to the Hanamaulu Chicken!"

—Paula Akana
*Television Anchor
and Community Volunteer*

Back

IN THE

Day

Enjoy Hawai'i's Comfort Foods from Family and Friends

Lynette Lo Tom

PHOTOGRAPHY BY
Kaz Tanabe

Mutual Publishing

Library of Congress Control Number: 2018951386

ISBN: 978-1939487-99-5

Photography © Kaz Tanabe, unless oherwise noted
Photography © Food Styling Hawai'i on pages 12, 30, 56, 76, 97, 109, 127
Photography © Malcom Mekaru and Olivier Koning on page 146 and cover
Photograph by Karin Hatcher on page 133
Photograph by Lynette Lo Tom on pages xi, 108, 112
Photographs from Lynette Lo Tom collection on pages iii, ix, x (all), 41, 66
Recipe cards and papers from Lorna Lo on pages 69, 93, 129, 138, 141
Design by Courtney Tomasu

First Printing, October 2018

Mutual Publishing, LLC
1215 Center Street, Suite 210
Honolulu, Hawaii 96816
Ph: 808-732-1709 / Fax: 808-734-4094
email: info@mutualpublishing.com
www.mutualpublishing.com

Printed in South Korea

Photographs from Dreamstime.com:
pg. vii (broccoli) © Nikmerkulov; pg. xiv (brown sugar) © Moonborne, (butter) © Sommai Sommai, (eggs) © Robyn Mackenzie, (soy sauce) © Baibaz; pg. 7 © Yong Hian Lim; pg. 11 © Manyakotic; pg. 14 © Ppy2010ha; pg. 15 (background) © Diane Behnke; pg. 19 © Joshua Resnick; pg. 26 © Aas2009; pg. 29 © Ppy2010ha; pg. 37 © Sriharun; pg. 40 © Brebca; pg. 58 © Penchan Pumila; pg. 61 © Alberto Grosescu; pg. 71 © Naruto4836; pg. 73 © Danelle Mccollum; pg. 82 © Msphotographic; pg. 86 © Brad Calkins; pg. 93 © Valery Kraynov; pg. 94 © Joseph Skompski; pg. 100 © Marilyn Barbone; pg. 106 © Panco971; pg. 112 © MarieMaerz; pg. 116 © Leigh Anne Meeks; pg. 117 © Enika; pg. 118 © Siraphol; pg. 120 © Winai Tepsuttinun; pg. 123 © Elena Veselova; pg. 128 © Charles Knowles; pg. 130 © Atide15; pg. 131 © Liliya Kandrashevich; pg. 132 © Dmitri Mihhailov; pg. 143 © Junyan Jiang; pg. 144 (daikon) © Le Thuy Do; pg. ©; pg. 145 (orange) © Valentyn75, (watercress) © Kewuwu

This cookbook is dedicated with love to my daughter,
Jenny Claire Lai Huerng Tom Lin. May you create your
own precious food memories with your son,
Theo David Lin.

Table of Contents

Beef and Lamb

Seafood and Fish

Side Dishes

Pork

Breads

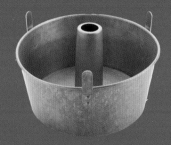

Desserts

Mahalo to Many

I pay honor to the wonderful cooks in my family. Mother Lorna Lee Lo, an inspiration. John Sau Lee and Florence Lee, Louise Ho Lo, Ethel Lo Ching, and Lillian "Eio" Lee Chu, all good cooks and bakers. Calabash Auntie Thelma Tomonari, who taught me to love Japanese food. Joanne Lo Grimes, Charlene Lo Chan, Russell Lo and Barry Lo, my siblings.

Two good friends, Taren Taguchi and Debbie Lau Okamura, have encouraged me for years and were convinced I could write a cookbook. Chefs Ed Kenney and Dave Caldiero keep teaching me how to make food taste better.

Special thanks to Taren Taguchi, Joyce Timpson, and Floyd Takeuchi for helping to proof this book.

The following are thanked for their generosity in sharing their precious recipes and memories:

Adrienne Yee
Ann Harakawa
Ann Yoshida
Arlen Lung
Arlene Sullivan
Barbara Tongg
Cheryl Bochentin
Didi and Wayne Iwaoka
Don Ojiri
Eleanor Nakama-Mitsunaga
Esther "Dede" Lo Chinn
Ethel Lo Ching
Ginger Lee Grimes
Gregg Hirata and Yukie Hirata
Hannah Chan
Helen Noh Lee
Janet Eckart
Jean Grimes
Jenny Tom Lin

Jooeun Kwak
Karen Fuse and Nora Chibana
Karin Hatcher
Keiko and Darrell Yamagata
Laura Thue
Lillian "Eio" Lee Chu
Lloyd and Diana Komagome
Lorna Lee Lo
Melinda and Eppie Lopez
Myrna Chun-Hoon
Nobuyo Kanda
Pam Leong
Priscilla Lau
Sue Youth
Taren Taguchi and Ben Taguchi
Terry Doan Shelton
   and Dudley Doan
Thelma Tomonari
Tina Chang

Those who donated their talents to help prepare the food or assist with the food photography are deeply appreciated:

Becky Choy
Cathy Tanaka
Christie Wilson
Courtney Mau
Debbie Lau Okamura
Frances Yuan-Hayashi
Herb Conley
Ida Elliott
Jean Nakanishi
Jimmy Leon
Julie Krucky
Karen Fuse
Karen Robertshaw
Lacy Matsumoto
Lani Parry

Malcolm Mekaru
Malie Moran
Maria Leon
Olivier Koning
Regino Ojano III
Robin Johns
Robyn Kuraoka
Roger Yu
Stephen Dung
Taren Taguchi
Vina Yamashiro
Wei Ping Lum

Mahalo to my editor, Betty Shimabukuro, and to those at Mutual Publishing, including:

Bennett Hymer
Courtney Tomasu
Gay Wong

Jane Gillespie
Kaz Tanabe

And most of all, I thank my husband, Neal Kanda, who is my secret weapon in life. He tastes my food every day and gives honest feedback on the taste and on my writing. I deeply appreciate his support of my love for food creativity.

As you can tell, this was a project made possible by many people. Please forgive me if I have forgotten to mention you.

Lynette

Introduction

Food is my expression of love. I am so lucky to come from a family that loves to eat. My "small kid" years were wonderful, filled with lots of home cooking and adventurous eating.

My mother, Lorna Lee Lo, was a terrific cook and showed me how rewarding cooking could be by requiring me to cook dinner from age eleven.

The 1960s and '70s were interesting times of change for housewives, my mother among them. New products—boxed cake mixes, a wide variety of canned goods, and frozen foods—provided shortcuts for getting tasty, filling meals to the table.

My mother, Lorna Lee Lo

When my parents went out at night, the unpleasantness of having a babysitter was offset by the treat of getting to eat a frozen TV dinner. I can still remember the fried chicken or Salisbury steak, peas or corn, mashed potatoes, and a soft apple cake.

As much as that was a novelty, the best food was the home cooking from my mother,

Popo (Grandmother) Louise Ho Lo

my paternal grandmother, Louise Ho Lo and my maternal grandfather, John Sau Lee.

In those days, grocery stores offered only a portion of what they do now, so cooking from scratch was not an option, but a necessity. Most households were proud of their freshly baked goods and home-cooked meals.

Florence and John Sau Lee (Japo and Goong Goong)

Milk was delivered to our front door, a yasai (vegetable) man came to our neighborhood selling produce, and we ran to find our coins when we heard the catchy melody of the ice cream truck driving down the street.

These days an occasional ice cream truck is all that brings us back to those long-ago times.

At eighty-eight, my mother no longer cooks. She has paid her dues by cooking for more than sixty years and I am happy now to step up. I have long wanted to write a cookbook that would keep my mother's recipes alive.

It is my hope that this book will take you back to a certain point in time, my mother's time, and that it will serve as a tribute to her skill and inventiveness in the kitchen.

Six years ago I scaled back my public relations and marketing company, Bright Light Marketing, to focus on cooking.

Soon after, Betty Shimabukuro, on behalf of the *Honolulu Star-Advertiser*, asked me to write a Chinese cookbook as part of the Hawai'i Cooks series on ethnic foods. I was thrilled to do so, and that resulted in *A Chinese Kitchen* cookbook, comprising many of my mother's recipes.

But my mother had many non-Chinese recipes, and in this book I am proud to share many of them. I am also so grateful to other relatives and friends who shared their signature dishes here.

When I cook these back-in-the-day recipes, I'm reminded of happy, unstructured times, when we would play outside with the neighbors on the street or in the stream until our mothers called us home for dinner. Almost every night, we would eat a tasty, home-cooked meal.

This book is also shaped by foods outside my family circle. At every gathering, mothers (mostly mothers in those days) would present their latest, greatest recipes. They would exchange recipes and then you would see that dish at the next get-together.

These days we have so much exposure to international foods. I remember joyfully discovering Mexican tacos in the fifth grade when a neighbor moved from the mainland—tacos were her favorite. I also enjoy Filipino, Puerto Rican, and Samoan foods, all discovered later in life.

I've included recipes that I find delicious, but cooking is very personal. Please try these recipes and adapt them to your own preferences. And please cook for those you love.

Life is short, so let's get cooking!

With aloha,

Lynette Lo Tom

Terms

Throughout this book, the meaning of certain terms is assumed, for example:

Brown sugar—should be measured by packing it down

Butter—unsalted

Done—in baking, use a cake tester, skewer, or toothpick. Insert into the bread or cake and remove. If it comes out clean, the cake is done. If batter sticks, continue cooking longer and test again.

Eggs—large size

Flour—all-purpose, versus bread flour or cake flour

Pepper—ground black

Oil—any vegetable oil, such as canola or peanut. Usually not olive oil, as it has a stronger flavor.

Salt—traditional table salt. Many people today prefer natural sea salt, kosher salt or Hawaiian rock salt, but in our family's traditional recipes, we used basic Morton's. If you prefer to use kosher salt, double the amount listed in the recipe.

Soy sauce—traditional, not low-salt or tamari

Sugar—white granulated

To taste—taste the dish and add flavorings as you prefer

Pūpū

This section comprises an assortment of pūpū, or appetizers, that you can prepare easily. They include a wonderful variety of my mother's favorites—basics like Hot Artichoke Dip and Deviled Eggs—to the more adventurous, like Chuba Iriko (Seasoned Dried Anchovies).

Remember when Rumaki was served at every party? The little marinated chicken liver, water chestnut, and bacon bites are due for a comeback!

Living in Mānoa Valley, we got to eat wonderful Japanese food—in those days, the area was populated mainly by Japanese Americans. Our favorite Japanese or Japanese-influenced foods include meatballs with teriyaki sauce, pickled cucumbers (namasu) with clams, and the crunchy dried anchovies.

We attended many fun potlucks at friends' homes or after a T-ball baseball game in the park. Those get-togethers were a chance to eat the best homemade appetizers. We would stay out late because the parents would have such a great time "talking story" and us kids would invent games.

Enjoy these recipes, which take me back to simpler times of great memories and laughter with family and neighbors.

Deviled Eggs

These may be old-fashioned but they are always the first appetizer to be eaten, perhaps because you can so easily pick them up with your fingers. Or they remind you of when you were young. Or because they are infrequently served. Whatever the reason, allow at least one egg per person attending your party. Don't say I didn't warn you to make enough.

12 eggs
½ cup mayonnaise (Best Foods preferred)
2 tablespoons sweet pickle relish
2 teaspoons dry hot mustard (Coleman's preferred)

1 teaspoon salt
1 teaspoon pepper
Optional: 1 tablespoon grated onion
Optional: Ground paprika or cayenne pepper

Hard boil eggs in the method you prefer. Here is one that works: Put the eggs in a pot and cover with water. Bring to boil on high and boil eggs 11 minutes. Immediately drop eggs into a cold-water bath, gently crack each one and return it to the bath. You may need to refresh the bath with cold water. Quickly peel each egg and cut in half lengthwise.

Scoop out yolks and place in a sieve. Push yolks through the screen to break them into small pieces and to eliminate any hard parts. Add mayonnaise, relish, mustard, salt and pepper. Add grated onion, if using. Chill yolk mixture and egg whites separately in the refrigerator until you are ready to serve.

Spoon the yolk mixture into the whites. Or put the yolk mixture in a plastic bag. Cut one corner off the bag and squeeze the mixture through the opening to fill the whites. Garnish with ground paprika for a mild taste, or cayenne pepper for a kick. Serve immediately or refrigerate again until the party starts.

Other suggested toppings: Small parsley leaf, ikura (salmon roe), smoked salmon, Sriracha sauce, capers, Portuguese Pickled Onions (see page 6), anchovies, or anything else you can imagine.

Pickled Vegetables, Ba-_Le_-Style

Makes about 1 cup

Ba-Le Sandwich Shops in Hawai'i feature the popular Vietnamese-French sandwich called banh mi. Assorted ingredients fill a French baguette, spiced up with slightly sweet pickled vegetables. This recipe approximates the taste of those pickles. I find them perfect to eat with crispy-skinned roast pork in a bao bun with hoisin sauce. Or serve them by themselves as a crunchy appetizer.

1 carrot, peeled
1 daikon (white radish), peeled
1 red or green bell pepper
¼ cup Hawaiian salt or fine sea
   salt

Pickling liquid:
¼ cup rice vinegar
1 tablespoon sugar
½ cup water

Cut carrot, daikon and pepper into strips ¼-inch wide by 2 inches long. Place in a colander and sprinkle with salt. Let drain at least 30 minutes.

Meanwhile, make pickling liquid: In a small pot, heat vinegar with sugar and water on low. Stir until sugar is dissolved. Cool.

Rinse salted vegetables in cold running water. Squeeze and place in a large bowl. Mix with cooled pickling liquid. Cover bowl with plastic wrap or transfer vegetables to an airtight container. If needed, place crumpled parchment or waxed paper on top of vegetables to keep the vegetables submerged. Let sit overnight unrefrigerated, then refrigerate.

Good by itself, or use in sandwiches.

My father claimed his sandwiches tasted better than others. His secret—one side of the bread had Best Foods mayonnaise and the other the sweeter Miracle Whip. He said the combination made his cold cut, cheese, and lettuce sandwiches the best. Most days he would take one sandwich to work. He would eat half at lunch and save the other half to give to the grandchild he was picking up from school.

Portuguese Pickled Onions

Makes 2 quarts

In some homes, these refreshing pickles are on the table for every meal. Make them with as much heat as you like by adding or subtracting chili peppers. The vinegary sweet onions are a good contrast with rich foods such as laulau or roasted meats.

5 pounds sweet onions (about 7),
 each cut into 4 or 6 wedges
1 garlic bulb, peeled and broken
 into cloves
1 bell pepper, sliced
2 bay leaves
3 Hawaiian chili peppers, sliced
 lengthwise and seeded

Pickling mix:
2 cups water
2 cups sugar
2 cups white or cider vinegar
2 cups Hawaiian salt

Pickles are one way of preserving vegetables. Vinegar, sugar, and salt work their magic. Fermented foods are as popular today as they were decades ago.

Combine onions, garlic, bell pepper, bay leaves and chilies in a nonreactive bowl or container. Combine pickling mix ingredients; do not heat. Pour over vegetables. Cover with a dishcloth or plastic wrap. Leave unrefrigerated overnight. Pack into containers with liquid and refrigerate. Ready to eat!

Cucumber Namasu with Clams

Makes about 2 cups

This is a very refreshing appetizer or an amuse bouche (a small treat at the start of a meal to symbolize what is to come). Hokkigai, or surf clams, are among the most expensive clams, but make a special treat. Do not add the clams to the pickled cucumbers (namasu) in advance or they will toughen and lose their flavor of the ocean. Scoring adds a pleasant design to the pickled cucumber slices.

4 Japanese cucumbers
1½ tablespoons salt
1 (7-ounce) can Hokkigai, or
   surf clams, liquid reserved (or
   substitute other canned clams)

Pickling sauce:
½ cup sugar
½ teaspoon salt
½ cup rice vinegar
1 tablespoon grated ginger

Wash cucumbers and cut off ends. Using a fork, score the skins lengthwise. Cut cucumber into ¼-inch rounds. Put in a bowl and add salt; let sit at least 30 minutes.

In a separate bowl, combine pickling sauce ingredients. Mix until sugar is dissolved. Set aside.

Drain cucumbers and squeeze out excess water. Do not rinse. Add cucumbers to pickling sauce with reserved liquid from clams. Mix and refrigerate at least one hour, or overnight. Just before serving, cut clams in ½-inch chunks and with pickled cucumbers.

Rumaki

Makes 20

This seemingly odd combination is just spectacular. Chicken livers, water chestnuts, and bacon are marinated, then broiled, to create an easy-to-eat finger food.

10 water chestnuts, cut in half
5 chicken livers, cleaned and quartered
10 slices bacon, cut in half
20 toothpicks

Marinade:
1 tablespoon white wine
¼ cup soy sauce
2 tablespoons brown sugar
½ teaspoon grated ginger

Wrap 1 piece of water chestnut with 1 piece of liver in a piece of bacon. Secure with a toothpick. Continue until all chestnut halves and liver pieces are wrapped. Combine marinade ingredients in bowl and mix thoroughly. Add wrapped water chestnuts/liver; marinate for 2 hours.

Broil in the oven until bacon is crisp and liver is cooked. Serve hot or at room temperature.

San Francisco chef Chris Cosentino has made cooking with offal famous. We grew up with it. My mother cooked calves' brains with scrambled eggs. We ate liver, onions and bacon, tripe, gizzards, stomach, and intestines. One reason is that Chinese eat all parts, but another is that in those days, you didn't want to waste anything.

Teriyaki Meatballs

Makes about 30 meatballs

This is a favorite party pūpū, popular with children.

½ **pound ground beef**
1 **egg**
2 **tablespoons bread crumbs**
2 **tablespoons chopped onions**
½ **teaspoon salt**
¼ **teaspoon pepper**

1 **tablespoon vegetable oil**
½ **cup soy sauce**
¼ **cup sugar**
1 **clove garlic, minced**
1 **teaspoon minced ginger**
Optional garnish: Sesame seeds

In a mixing bowl, combine beef, egg, bread crumbs, onions, salt, and pepper. Shape into ¾-inch balls, using a small ice cream scoop if you have one. In a large skillet, heat oil and brown meatballs in batches over medium heat for 5 minutes. Add soy sauce, sugar, garlic, and ginger to the skillet. Continue cooking until done, about 20 minutes, turning meatballs often. Garnish with sesame seeds. Enjoy hot or at room temperature.

Chuba Iriko
(Seasoned Dried Anchovies)

Serves 4 to 6 as an appetizer

These crunchy, tasty, small fish are addictive. Make them ahead of time and bring them out as pūpū (appetizers). The sweet and salty flavors make them a perfect complement to beer.

2 **(3-ounce) packages of chuba iriko (dried anchovies)**
½ **cup soy sauce**
3 **tablespoons sugar**

2 **tablespoons toasted sesame seeds**
1 **teaspoon dried chili peppers or crushed fresh peppers**

Preheat oven to 350°F. Put chuba iriko on baking sheet; bake 15 to 20 minutes.

In a small pot, combine remaining ingredients and bring to simmer. Pour over hot fish and toss. Serve immediately or cool and refrigerate. Bring to room temperature before serving.

Japanese-Style Kim Chee

Makes about 5 cups

This recipe is from Darrell Yamagata, who learned it from his mother, Keiko. It is sweeter than Korean kim chee and includes salted sliced kelp. The combination will be a winning offering at your dinner table or at parties. The vinegar and salt will shrink the vegetables, so while it may seem that you are making too much, you will end up with a much smaller amount. Eat this on the first day when it's mild or keep it in the refrigerator, where it will ferment and grow in strength. Modify this dish with the vegetable mix of your choice.

4 pounds Japanese cucumber, score skin lengthwise with a fork, cut in half lengthwise then slice into ½-inch half moons
1 large head cabbage, cut into 1-inch chunks (about 10 cups)
1 large daikon (white radish), peeled and cut into ¼-inch half moons (about 3 cups),
¾ cup Hawaiian salt

Kim chee sauce:
1 cup rice vinegar
¾ cup sugar
¾ cup kim chee base (Momoya brand preferred)

1 (1.4-ounce) package shiofuki konbu (salted sliced kelp)

Place vegetables in separate bowls. Mix salt in vegetables and let sit at room temperature for at least 3 hours or overnight. The denser daikon may take longer to wilt. Rinse vegetables of salt; squeeze to remove as much water as possible. Set aside.

Combine kim chee sauce ingredients; mix. Add drained vegetables; stir. Taste. If salty enough, rinse shiofuki konbu, drain and add. If it needs more salt, add the konbu in without rinsing. Eat right away or refrigerate.

Hot Artichoke Dip

Serves 8 to 10

This is one of my mother's favorites to prepare for a party. It gets eaten very quickly.

1 (14-ounce) can non-marinated artichoke hearts or pieces, rinsed, drained, and roughly chopped
¾ cup grated Parmesan cheese
1 cup mayonnaise (Best Foods preferred)

3 cloves garlic, minced
2 tablespoons minced onion
Dash Tabasco sauce
Dash Worcestershire sauce
½ teaspoon cayenne pepper, plus additional for garnish

Preheat oven to 350°F. Combine all ingredients, except cayenne, and place in a heat-proof casserole dish. Sprinkle with cayenne (this should not be omitted as it adds the needed kick). Bake uncovered for 35 minutes. Serve immediately with crackers or sliced French bread.

Variation: Add a drained can of crab to the mix or 1 (4.5-ounce) can of green chilies.

Salads and Soups

When we were young, salads and salad dressings were made from scratch. I see a return to that now as people want to know their ingredients. The classic Tropics and Easy French dressings in this chapter can help a novice learn to get along without bottled salad dressings.

But dressings are just the start. Try a creative full salad such as the Big Island favorite of warabi, made with local fern shoots, or a throwback such as the pea salad so popular at Ryan's Grill and Horatio's.

With so many choices for fresh ingredients, please take advantage of the bounty to assemble a salad.

When you prefer a simple, hot entree, make Corn Chowder. It seems to be our state's favorite soup, especially with children. And the Korean staple of Seaweed Soup is healthy and satisfying.

Doing it yourself brings fresh and satisfying results.

Warabi Salad

Serves 8 as a side dish

Good cook and longtime friend Taren Taguchi shared this recipe from her late father, Ben, who created his version of a Hilo favorite. Tender fern shoots are called hō'i'o in Hawaiian, or warabi in Japanese. The combination is very refreshing and addictive.

1 bunch (3 to 4 inches in diameter) warabi (hō'i'o)
2 teaspoons salt
3 ounces dried shredded codfish
1 (1.4-ounce) package shiofuki konbu (salted dried kelp strips)
½ onion, thinly sliced
½ (5.5-ounce) block kamaboko (Japanese fish cake), julienned

3 tomatoes, roughly diced (¾-inch) or 15 to 20 grape tomatoes, chopped
5 ounces firm tofu, drained and cut into ½-inch squares

Dressing:
¼ cup brown sugar
1½ tablespoons sesame oil
1 tablespoon soy sauce
1 tablespoon white vinegar

Wash warabi and cut into 1½-inch pieces. Separate the stems from the tender tops. In a pot large enough to hold the warabi, boil water and add salt. Place the stems in the pot and let cook 1½ minutes. Turn off heat. Use a spider scoop or slotted spoon to remove warabi from pot into a bowl of ice and water to stop the cooking (this eliminates the gooeyness of the plant). Remove stems from ice bath and place in large mixing bowl, but keep the cold liquid and any remaining ice.

Water in pot will still be hot; add warabi tops and let blanch for 30 seconds. Drain and add to ice bath. Once cool, drain and add to mixing bowl. Pat dry.

Rinse codfish in running water and strip thinner, if desired. Add to warabi. Shake off excess salt from konbu. Add konbu, onion, and kamaboko to bowl.

In a small bowl, combine dressing ingredients; mix thoroughly.

Add dressing and tomatoes to warabi mixture; stir. Gently mix in tofu. Cover bowl and refrigerate at least 2 hours. Enjoy cold.

Note: Substitute prepared taegu for the dried codfish.

Caesar Salad

Serves 6

It's amazing that this salad has been a favorite in Hawai'i for at least fifty years. It probably was popular on the mainland for at least double that time, although invented in Mexico in the 1920s.

I attribute that to the saltiness of the anchovies and cheese, as well as the fresh lemon taste. Do not try to save time by cutting the romaine leaves. Tearing them makes the salad more interesting. Also, do not discard the stems, they add a needed crunch. Use the best Parmesan cheese you can find and grate it yourself. The ingredients are simple, so each one should be the highest quality you can afford to make this a classic for the next fifty years.

Dressing:
1 (2-ounce) can anchovies in oil
2 large cloves garlic, minced
½ cup salad oil
1 egg, coddled (see note below)
1 tablespoon Worcestershire sauce
1 dash Tabasco sauce
¼ cup fresh lemon juice
½ teaspoon pepper
½ teaspoon salt

8 cups torn romaine lettuce, washed and dried (do not cut with a knife)
½ cup grated Parmesan cheese
Optional: 2 tablespoons mint leaves, sliced
1 cup croutons (recipe follows)

To make dressing: Drain anchovies and cut into pieces. In a large bowl, mix anchovies, garlic, oil, egg, Worcestershire sauce, Tabasco, lemon juice, pepper, and salt. Dressing may be made ahead and refrigerated.

Place torn romaine lettuce in a large salad bowl; toss with dressing. Mix in cheese and mint leaves, if using, and top with croutons. Serve immediately.

Note:

How to coddle an egg: You may prefer to use pasteurized eggs. They are more expensive, but are available in grocery stores. Bring a small pot of water to a boil. Gently lower an egg into water and let cook 1 minute. Remove; crack open. If you are uncomfortable about adding a coddled egg, substitute 1 tablespoon mayonnaise.

Croutons

1 (14-ounce) loaf dense Italian or French bread, cut into ¾-inch cubes
½ cup butter
¼ cup olive oil

2 teaspoons salt
8 large cloves garlic, minced
½ cup minced flat leaf parsley
3 tablespoons grated Parmesan cheese

Cut bread and set aside.

In a saucepan, melt butter over low heat. Add olive oil, salt, and garlic. Simmer about 5 minutes.

Preheat oven to 350°F. Put bread on a foil-covered baking sheet; toss with butter mixture. Bake 30 to 35 minutes, until crunchy, stirring once or twice. Remove from oven; top with parsley and cheese while hot. Cool. Store remainder in an airtight container.

Waldorf Salad

Serves 8 to 10

This classic fruit-and-nuts salad is enjoyed cold. What apples are the best to use? My mother would advise, "Whatever apple is on sale," or "Whatever you have in your ice box!" She, like many others of her generation, was practical and tried to feed many on a budget.

¾ cup walnuts or pecans, whole, halves or pieces
4 crisp apples, Pippin, McIntosh, Fuji or Envy, peeled and cored
Juice of 1 lemon
1 cup finely diced celery
¼ cup diced red bell pepper
3 green onions, finely chopped
Optional: 1 to 2 heads Mānoa or Bibb lettuce

Dressing:
¾ cup mayonnaise (Best Foods preferred)
1 tablespoon Dijon mustard
1½ tablespoons honey
1 teaspoon minced fresh mint leaves
Salt and pepper, to taste

Preheat oven to 200°F. Spread nuts on a foil-lined baking sheet; bake until nuts are toasted, 5 to 7 minutes. Cool, chop, and set aside.

Dice apples into ½-inch pieces. Place in a large mixing bowl; add lemon juice. Add celery, bell pepper, green onions, and toasted nuts; mix.

In another bowl, combine dressing ingredients, adding salt and pepper last. Add to apple mixture. Serve immediately or refrigerate for 1 hour.

Separate, wash, and dry the lettuce leaves, if using. Arrange around a large platter. Spoon salad into middle of leaves and serve.

In Hawai'i we like mayonnaise. The preferred brand is Best Foods. Your friends on the East Coast know the same condiment as Hellmann's.

Spinach Salad

Serves 4 to 6

In the 1960s and '70s, a spinach salad was an elegant addition to dinner. Somehow the rich bacon fat combined with the tartness of vinegar and the spinach make an addictive salad. The amount of spinach seems too much, but the leaves will wilt because of the vinegar and salt.

4 pounds fresh spinach leaves
½ medium onion, finely chopped
1 clove garlic, minced
⅓ cup olive oil
⅓ cup apple cider vinegar
½ teaspoon salt

½ teaspoon pepper
½ pound bacon, cut in ½-inch pieces
1 tablespoon sugar
2 hard-boiled eggs, peeled and chopped

Wash spinach leaves carefully to remove any grit. Pat dry and remove any tough stems. Leave small leaves whole, but tear larger ones in half or quarter them. Place in a large salad bowl.

Mix onion, garlic, olive oil, vinegar, salt, and pepper in a separate bowl; set aside.

In a skillet, cook bacon until crisp. Pour about half the grease out of the pan. You can save half of the bacon grease for another dish. Add oil and vinegar mixture to the remaining bacon fat in pan. Bring this mixture to a boil and let it cook for a few seconds.

Pour hot mixture over the spinach quickly; toss gently. Sprinkle with sugar and mix again gently. Top with eggs and serve immediately.

Today we are conscious of how much processed meat we consume, but back in the day it was common to eat Spam, luncheon meat, bacon, Vienna sausage, corned beef hash, hot dogs, all types of sausages and bologna. My father, Richard Lo, liked to cook bologna for breakfast, making four slits in the round meat, so it would fry flat in the cast-iron pan.

Pea Salad

Serves 8

Every Thanksgiving, my mother would make this salad and everyone loved it. She claims the reasons are: 1. Bacon is included and 2. The peas are crunchy because you do not cook them, you just defrost them. It reminds many of the Broadway pea salad served at Horatio's, which became Kincaid's, and Ryan's Grill—both restaurants once located in Kaka'ako.

8 slices bacon
4 cups frozen peas, defrosted but not cooked
1 cup mayonnaise
½ cup sour cream

1 (8-ounce) can water chestnuts, chopped
½ cup chopped onion
1 teaspoon pepper
2 cups slivered snow peas
Salt to taste

Fry or bake bacon until crisp. My mother would save the bacon fat for another use such as sautéing vegetables. Chop bacon and set aside.

In a large bowl, mix peas, mayonnaise, sour cream, water chestnuts, onion, and pepper. Add ¾ of the bacon, then snow peas. Season with salt. Refrigerate at least 1 hour. Just before serving, garnish with remaining bacon.

Note: If omitting bacon, add ½ teaspoon salt and garnish with an additional ⅛ cup of slivered snow peas.

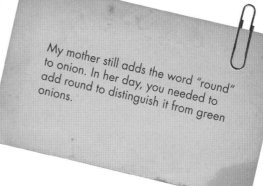

My mother still adds the word "round" to onion. In her day, you needed to add round to distinguish it from green onions.

Soba Salad

Adapted from a recipe from our friend, Karen Fuse, who learned it from her mother, Nora Chibana. This recipe is easily doubled.

¼ cup hijiki seaweed, soaked in water for 20 minutes
1 tablespoon soy sauce
1 tablespoon sugar
9 ounces dried soba noodles, cooked according to package instructions
1 bunch watercress or spinach, cut into 2-inch pieces (about 4 cups), tough stems discarded
¼ sweet onion, thinly sliced
¼ pound ocean salad
1 (4-ounce) package radish sprouts, roots removed, cut in 2-inch slices

1 (5.5-ounce) kamaboko (fish cake), cut into strips
1 Japanese cucumber, cut into strips
¼ cup takuan (pickled daikon), cut into strips

Dressing:
2½ tablespoons vegetable oil
6 tablespoons soy sauce
2 tablespoons sugar
3 tablespoons fresh lemon juice

After soaking the hijiki seaweed, rinse and drain. Squeeze to eliminate all water. In a saucepan over medium heat, cook hijiki with 1 tablespoon soy sauce and 1 tablespoon sugar until liquid is absorbed.

Layer salad ingredients in a 9 x 13-inch dish or bowl, in order listed. Combine dressing ingredients and pour over salad just before serving.

Variations: Add red or pink sliced pickled ginger, different types of Japanese fish cake, prepared taegu (codfish), use surimi (imitation crab) instead of kamaboko.

Antipasto Salad

Serves 6

Family friend Janet Eckart of Boulder, Colorado, taught us how to make this Italian-style vegetable appetizer.

1 head cauliflower, broken into
  florets and briefly parboiled
3 stalks celery, sliced into ½-inch
  pieces, parboiled
1 green pepper, cored and diced
1 (6-ounce) jar pitted black olives,
  drained
1 (6-ounce) jar green olives,
  drained
1 (4-ounce) jar pimentos, drained
Optional: Artichoke hearts
Optional: Fresh mushrooms

<u>Mustard dressing:</u>
1 tablespoon Dijon mustard
1 tablespoon parsley
1½ teaspoon salt
1½ teaspoon sugar
1 teaspoon pepper
1 large clove garlic, smashed
¼ cup olive oil
¼ cup red wine vinegar
1 teaspoon dried oregano

Combine dressing ingredients in a large bowl. Add vegetables. Cover and refrigerate overnight.

Easy French Dressing

Auntie Barbara Lee Tongg taught my mother to make this very simple and quick salad dressing. When we were growing up, it seemed everyone made their own dressings. Today, I see a resurgence of that as people seek to control the ingredients in the food they eat, and to eliminate additives.

⅓ cup ketchup
⅓ cup white vinegar
⅓ cup oil
⅓ cup sugar, substitute honey or
 agave syrup

½ teaspoon Worcestershire sauce
¼ teaspoon salt
¼ teaspoon pepper
¼ teaspoon granulated garlic,
 optional

Mix ingredients and chill at least 30 minutes before serving.

Tropics Dressing

Makes 3 cups

This is a retro salad dressing that is good with just vegetables, or in a salad with crab, turkey, or tuna added.

1⅔ cups oil
1 cup ketchup
½ cup mayonnaise (Best Foods
 preferred)
½ cup sugar
2 teaspoons salt
2 tablespoons wine vinegar

¾ teaspoon hot dry mustard, such
 as Coleman's
1 teaspoon Worcestershire sauce
1 teaspoon A.1. Sauce
Juice of 1 lemon
1 large clove garlic, minced

Mix all ingredients and refrigerate at least 1 hour before serving.

Coleslaw

Serves 6

What is a summer picnic without coleslaw? Even children will eat their vegetables this way. Chop vegetables finely if you want to mimic the coleslaw served at KFC.

8 cups cabbage, finely sliced or chopped
2 carrots, peeled and finely grated

Dressing:
¾ cup mayonnaise (Best Foods preferred)
¼ cup cider vinegar
1 tablespoon sugar
1 teaspoon celery salt
½ teaspoon freshly ground pepper
¼ teaspoon salt

In a mixing bowl, combine dressing ingredients. Add cabbage and carrots; mix. Refrigerate at least 4 hours.

Carrot-Apple-Raisin Salad

Serves 6

I think this refreshing salad—a standard dish of the 1960s and '70s— is due for a comeback. It's great for your vegetarian friends.

1 cup shredded carrots
3 cups apples, diced
⅓ cup raisins
⅓ cup walnuts, chopped

⅔ cup mayonnaise (Best Foods preferred)
1 tablespoon fresh lemon juice
¼ teaspoon salt

Combine all ingredients and refrigerate at least 2 hours before serving.

Korean Seaweed Soup

Serves 12 or more

Jooeun Kwak was generous in sharing her family's recipe with our family twenty years ago. It is a light soup and you'll feel healthy eating the seaweed vegetable. At the Korean markets, ask for the type of seaweed for soup.

Handful (about 3 × 3-inches) dried wakame seaweed
½ pound flank steak, finely chopped so it resembles hamburger
1 tablespoon sesame oil

12 cups water, divided
1 tablespoon fish sauce
1 clove garlic, minced
1 teaspoon dashi (powdered soup base)
Salt to taste

In a bowl, soak seaweed in water for 30 minutes. Wash carefully under running water to eliminate any grit. Using scissors, cut into bite-sized pieces. Drain well.

In a large pot over medium heat, brown the meat in sesame oil, about 5 minutes. Add the drained seaweed and stir continuously for 10 minutes.

Add 2 cups water and let cook 10 to 15 minutes, until soup thickens. Add remaining 10 cups of water and let it come to boil. Add fish sauce, garlic, dashi, and salt; lower heat to simmer and cook 30 to 45 minutes longer. Cut seaweed again with scissors, if needed, as it will expand during cooking. Enjoy hot.

Variation: Substitute abalone for the flank steak.

Corn Chowder

Serves 4 to 6

Eleanor Nakama-Mitsunaga shared her family's recipe for their ever-popular hearty corn chowder.

8 to 10 slices bacon, chopped
1 large onion, chopped
2 tablespoons flour
2 (14.5-ounce) cans chicken broth
2 large potatoes, peeled and diced
1 (14.75-ounce) can cream-style corn

2 (11-ounce) cans sweet corn, drained
2 cups half-and-half, or substitute evaporated milk
1 teaspoon sugar
1 teaspoon garlic salt
½ teaspoon pepper

On high heat, fry bacon in large pot until brown. Skim oil if desired. Reduce heat to medium and add onions. Cook until translucent, about 5 minutes. Add flour and mix for 2 minutes. Add chicken broth and potatoes. Cook until potatoes are almost cooked, about 10 minutes.

Add canned corn and half-and-half or milk. Add sugar, garlic salt, and pepper. Cook until soup thickens and potatoes are fully cooked. Serve hot.

Variation: You could add fresh corn kernels from 7 to 8 cobs of corn and omit the two types of canned corn.

Poultry

My daughter Jenny often asked my mother to make her Turkey ala King. The old-fashioned creamy casserole combines leftover turkey or chicken with peas, pimentos, mushrooms, and onions. My mother didn't use a recipe, she just combined the ingredients by memory. We've put it all down into a recipe now, though, so Jenny can make it for her family.

Turkey and chicken were favorite proteins for my family. Many recipes here are from my family and close friends, and some are from well-loved restaurants. Several of those restaurants are no longer in business, but they live on through their dishes.

The Pottery restaurant on Wai'alae Avenue in Kaimukī was popular for its poultry served in ceramic dishes. We have their recipe for Cornish Game Hen with a memorable sauce.

Kaua'i's Hanamaulu Café is shuttered, but the fried chicken is legendary. The chicken absorbs the delicious taste from the marinade, then gets crispy from frying. What could be better?

Wisteria restaurant was at the mauka Diamond Head-corner of Pi'ikoi and King Streets. I still miss their Chicken Eggplant and 'Ahi Belly with Chiri Sauce (see page 83 for recipe).

In my mother's and grandmother's time, chicken was as pricey as beef. Now poultry is considered an inexpensive basic. So you can prepare these recipes for your family and still stay on budget.

Chicken Tetrazzini

Serves 8 to 10

Longtime friend Ann Yoshida makes this addictive casserole. It sounds Italian, but really is an American invention, mild-flavored and creamy.

4½ pounds chicken thighs, cut-up whole chicken, or chicken breasts—your preference
1 teaspoon salt
1 teaspoon onion salt
1½ teaspoons celery salt
½ pound dry spaghetti
6 tablespoons butter, divided
8 ounces mushrooms, sliced

1 tablespoon lemon juice
½ teaspoon salt
½ cup flour
1¼ teaspoons paprika
¼ teaspoon pepper
⅛ teaspoon nutmeg
1 cup heavy cream
⅔ cup Parmesan cheese
Garnish: Paprika

In a large pot, combine chicken, salt, onion salt, celery salt, and enough water to cover the chicken. Cover and cook on medium heat until chicken is fork tender, about 80 minutes.

Remove chicken from pot, leaving the broth in the pot. Debone chicken and remove skin; set aside.

Preheat oven to 400°F. Remove 2½ cups of the broth from the pot; set aside. To the remaining broth, add 3 quarts water; bring to a boil. Add spaghetti and cook 6 minutes; drain. Mix spaghetti and chicken in a large bowl.

In a skillet, melt 3 tablespoons butter. Add mushrooms, lemon juice, and salt. On medium heat, sauté until soft, but not brown. Add to the spaghetti and chicken.

In the same skillet, melt remaining 3 tablespoons butter and remove from heat. Stir in flour, paprika, pepper, and nutmeg. Slowly stir in the reserved chicken broth. Return to stove and cook on medium heat until thickened. Turn off heat and add cream. Mix with the spaghetti and chicken.

Put entire mixture into a large casserole dish; top with cheese and paprika, then cover with lid or foil. Bake 25 to 30 minutes.

(continued on the next page)

POULTRY

Note: This casserole may be prepared ahead, then covered with plastic wrap and refrigerated. When ready to bake, remove from refrigerator and let sit 20 minutes to take chill off. Bake at 400°F for 30 to 40 minutes, until heated through.

Variation: Substitute turkey for the chicken.

Chicken Broccoli Casserole

Serves 8 to 10

In Minnesota, Jean Grimes' home state, they call this "a hot dish." It's a great way to feed a large, hungry family. Her son Tom (my brother-in-law) says to make it a Minnesota treat, top this with tater tots before baking!

2 pounds chicken meat (boil a 3- to 4-pound chicken and discard bones and skin)
16 ounces fresh or frozen broccoli, blanched
2 (10.5-ounce) cans cream of chicken soup
1 cup mayonnaise
1 teaspoon curry powder
1 teaspoon lemon juice
1 cup breadcrumbs
2 tablespoons butter, melted
1 cup grated cheddar cheese

Preheat oven to 350°F. Cut up chicken and place in a 9 x 13-inch baking pan or large casserole dish. Arrange broccoli on top of chicken.

In a bowl, mix the condensed soup, mayonnaise, curry powder, and lemon juice. Pour over the chicken and broccoli. Bake uncovered for 30 minutes.

Mix breadcrumbs with butter. Remove casserole from oven and sprinkle with cheese. Top with breadcrumb and butter mixture. Return to oven and bake for 15 minutes longer. Serve hot or at room temperature.

Chicken Nishime

Japanese-Style Stew
Serves 15 to 20

This recipe is delicious even if you omit the chicken. It's a wonderful way to eat more vegetables. Many people leave out the round or oval araimo (Japanese taro) as it is time-consuming to cook and peel. But I find araimo to be one of the loveliest ingredients. Fresh araimo has a nice firm texture, but frozen araimo is usually mushy.

- 1 (3- to 4-pound) chicken, skin on, cut into pieces
- 3 tablespoons oil
- 2 carrots, peeled and cut into bite-sized pieces or sliced thinly and cut into flower designs using a metal vegetable cutter
- 2 cups gobo (burdock root), peeled and cut diagonally into 1-inch pieces
- 1 section hasu (lotus root), peeled and cut into ¼-inch slices, then quartered
- 1 (9-ounce) bag of konnyaku (yam jell), cut into ¼-inch slices, then slit down the middle lengthwise and twisted inside out
- 4 pieces aburage (deep-fried tofu pockets), cut into 1-inch wedges

- 1 (8.5-ounce) can bamboo shoots, rinsed and cut diagonally into bite-sized pieces
- 8 shiitake mushrooms, dried or fresh (if dried, soak in water until soft, stems discarded and quartered)
- 10 araimo (Japanese taro), blanched, then peeled
- 1 large daikon (white radish), peeled and cut into ¼-inch bite-sized pieces
- 1 (0.7-ounce) packet nishime konbu (seaweed), soaked in water for 30 minutes, cut into 1-inch wide strips and tied into individual knotted pieces
- ½ cup snow peas or sugar snap peas, strings removed

Sauce:
- ⅔ cups soy sauce
- 4 tablespoons mirin (sweet rice wine)
- 3 tablespoons sake
- 6 tablespoons sugar

- 1 teaspoon salt
- 1-inch ginger, peeled and cut into thin slices
- 5 cups chicken broth or water

(continued on the next page)

POULTRY

In a large pot, brown chicken pieces in oil over medium-high heat, about 10 minutes.

Combine sauce ingredients and add to pot. Cook 15 minutes on medium heat.

Skim oil. Add hardest vegetables first—carrots, gobo, and hasu; cook for 5 minutes. Then add konnyaku, aburage, bamboo shoots, shiitake mushrooms, and araimo, daikon, and konbu pieces. Cook for 5 minutes.

Add peas and cook for another 5 minutes. Do not overcook. Serve immediately hot or at room temperature.

Fried Chicken Thighs with Spicy Sauce

Serves 15 or more

Thelma Tomonari, mother of Al, Paul, Susan, and Myra, was a terrific cook. She was a whiz at preparing Japanese food and could make anything taste good. Here is one of her recipes. The fried chicken pieces are covered with a tasty dipping sauce.

Vegetable oil for frying
2 cups flour
1 tablespoon salt
5 pounds boneless chicken thighs, skin on or skinless

Dipping sauce:
1 cup soy sauce
1 cup sugar
4 garlic cloves, finely chopped
3 Hawaiian chili peppers, finely chopped
¼ cup chopped green onions

Heat oil in skillet to 350°F. Mix flour and salt in a bowl. Dredge each piece of chicken in flour; deep-fry over medium-high heat until cooked, about 10 minutes. Drain chicken on paper towels or a metal rack.

To make dipping sauce: Combine ingredients in a bowl. While chicken is still hot, dip in sauce and serve immediately or take to a party.

Barbecue Honey Lemon Chicken

Serves 4 to 6

One of the best things about living in Hawai'i is being able to enjoy the outdoors almost all year round. Here is a chicken recipe that takes the cooking outside and makes good use of the grill.

Sauce:
6 tablespoons butter
1 large clove garlic, minced
1 tablespoon onion juice (see note)
Grated zest of 1 lemon
Juice from 1 lemon
¼ cup steak sauce, like A.1. Sauce
1 tablespoon Worcestershire sauce

6 chicken legs (thighs and drumsticks)
3 tablespoons salad oil
¼ cup honey

To make sauce: In a large pot, simmer the butter, garlic, onion juice, lemon zest, lemon juice, steak sauce, and Worcestershire sauce until thickened, about 10 minutes. Cool for 15 minutes. Add chicken and refrigerate overnight.

Before barbecuing, bring sauce and chicken to room temperature. Rub oil on chicken. Barbecue over low heat until chicken is cooked, at least 40 minutes. Baste chicken continuously with sauce. After 30 minutes, add honey to the marinade and continue to baste. Serve hot or at room temperature.

In Hawai'i, many prefer the thighs or drumsticks over chicken breasts. It's a contrast to the mainland where restaurants charge more for all white meat.

Note: Onion juice is made by grating onions then measuring the liquid that results.

Chicken Eggplant

Serves 4

I miss the Wisteria restaurant that was on the mauka-Diamond Head side of the King and Pi'ikoi street intersection. It served homestyle Japanese and Okinawan food. We would order grilled 'ahi belly or chicken eggplant. Here is a nostalgic recipe.

1 pound boneless chicken thighs, sliced
1 cup soy sauce
4 tablespoons sugar
1 cup chicken broth
2 teaspoons sake

1½ cups dashi (see note below)
1¾ pounds Japanese eggplant, cut diagonally into ¾-inch slices
¼ cup string beans, blanched and cut diagonally into thin slices

In a skillet, add chicken then soy sauce, sugar, broth, sake, and dashi. Simmer over medium heat until chicken is cooked, about 10 to 15 minutes.

Add eggplant and cook until eggplant is tender, about 5 minutes. Garnish with string beans.

Note: Dashi can be made by mixing water with store-bought packets of dashi powder. You can choose from seaweed, shrimp, or bonito (aku) types and msg or non-msg varieties. The traditional way is to simmer dashi konbu (kelp) in warm water with bonito flakes. The kelp and fish flakes are discarded and the broth is used in cooking.

Hanamaulu Cafè Chicken

Makes enough to take to a party

The now-shuttered Hanamaulu Café was beloved by many on Kaua'i and its food was legendary. Here is a recipe that claims to duplicate the delicious chicken. It is similar to mochiko chicken in that the meat is marinated, then fried.

5 pounds chicken thighs, deboned and cut into bite-sized pieces
½ cup flour
½ cup cornstarch
2 cups vegetable oil

Marinade:
½ cup soy sauce
½ cup sugar
2 teaspoons sesame oil
1 teaspoon oyster sauce
1 teaspoon vinegar
1 teaspoon whiskey, substitute any liquor
1 teaspoon salt
¼ teaspoon ginger powder
¼ teaspoon garlic powder

Combine marinade ingredients and pour over chicken. Cover and refrigerate overnight.

In a deep fryer or large pot, heat oil to 350°F. Combine flour and cornstarch on a plate or using a bag. Remove chicken from marinade and dredge in flour-cornstarch mixture. Deep-fry in batches over medium-high heat until cooked, about 5 minutes. Serve hot or at room temperature.

Note: Update the taste by replacing ginger and garlic powder with ½ teaspoon grated ginger and ½ teaspoon minced garlic.

Rotisserie (Huli Huli) Chicken

Serves 16 to 20

Priscilla Lau created a dish that is similar to the popular island-style marinated, roasted chicken. Who can resist that smoky, sweet, and salty smell of grilled chicken?

4 chickens, cut in half
or 12 pounds of chicken thighs
¼ cup Hawaiian salt

Marinade:
½ cup soy sauce
½ cup lemon juice
½ cup oil
2 tablespoons sugar
1 large clove, crushed

Rub chickens with Hawaiian salt. Do not remove salt. Combine marinade ingredients; pour over chickens and marinate at least 30 minutes, but best overnight. Turn frequently so marinade covers all the chicken.

Barbecue until cooked or bake in the oven at 350°F for about 1 hour.

Mochiko Chicken

Serves 8 to 10

Arlen Lung shared this recipe with her sister Taren Taguchi, a dear classmate of mine, and it is the best. For a stronger flavor, marinate the chicken overnight.

2 pounds chicken thighs, deboned and skinned, cut into 1½-inch pieces
Vegetable oil for deep-frying

Coating:
2 tablespoons mochiko (sweet rice flour)
¼ cup cornstarch
¼ cup sugar
5 tablespoons soy sauce
½ teaspoon salt
2 eggs, beaten
¼ cup chopped green onions
2 cloves garlic, minced

Mix the coating ingredients. Add chicken and mix to coat well. Refrigerate at least 4 hours or overnight.

Heat oil in deep fryer, deep pot or skillet to 350°F. Fry chicken pieces in batches over medium heat. Drain on paper towels or a metal rack. Serve hot or at room temperature.

(L-R) My sister Charlene Chan, me, my mother Lorna Lo, and sister Joanne Grimes in the 1970s at Moanalua Gardens.

Nobu's Chicken Hekka

Serves 4 to 6

My mother-in-law, Nobuyo Kanda, was known for her chicken hekka. It's a popular dish and isn't difficult to prepare, but it is satisfying and comforting with all of its varied ingredients. My husband says his mother's version was tasty because it was sweet. Here is my attempt to duplicate her dish.

2 pounds chicken, bone-in or boneless
2 tablespoons vegetable oil
1 (20-ounce) can bamboo shoots, cut into bite-sized pieces
5 dried shiitake mushrooms, rehydrated in warm water and quartered, stems removed
1 (9-ounce) package konnyaku (yam jell), cut in ¼-inch slices
1 (7-ounce) package shirataki (yam jell noodles), can substitute long-rice noodles

1 large onion, cut in slices
¾ cup soy sauce
¾ cup sugar
½ cup chicken stock
¼ pound Napa cabbage, cut into 1-inch lengths
½ pound watercress, cut into 1½-inch lengths
10 green onions, cut into 1½-inch lengths

Remove skin and fat from chicken. Cut into bite-sized pieces. Brown chicken in oil in a large saucepan for about 10 minutes.

Add bamboo shoots, mushrooms, konnyaku, shirataki, onion, soy sauce, sugar, and chicken stock. Cover and simmer for 5 minutes.

Add Napa cabbage, watercress, and green onions. Simmer 5 more minutes. Serve immediately with hot rice.

Tip: After cutting the konnyaku in ¼-inch slices, cut through the rectangle lengthwise, leaving ¼-inch at the top and bottom. Turn it inside-out and you'll have a pretty pattern of konnyaku as seen on the top of the bowl in the photo (left).

Easy Cornish Game Hen

Serves 4 to 8

2 cups chicken broth
¾ cup soy sauce
¾ cup sugar

4 Cornish game hens, whole or cut in half

In a large pot or Dutch oven, combine broth, soy sauce, and sugar; bring to boil and cook until thickened, about 5 minutes.

Add game hens, cover and continue cooking on low heat until cooked, about 40 minutes. The hens will be dark brown.

The Pottery Cornish Game Hen with Sauce

Serves 2

The Pottery was a popular restaurant in Kaimukī where game hens were served in ceramic pottery pieces. One preparation used this sauce.

2 Cornish game hens

Sauce:
2 cups red wine
½ cup currant jelly
1 (15-ounce) can grapes in syrup
1 (14.5-ounce) can chicken stock
2 teaspoons salt
2 teaspoons pepper

Heat oven to 400°F. Bake hens 1 hour, until cooked through.

To make sauce: In a saucepan, boil wine until alcohol evaporates, about 10 minutes. Add jelly, grapes, chicken stock, salt, and pepper; simmer 10 minutes.

Place hens on a platter and cover with sauce.

Turkey Ala King

Serves about 20

This is a favorite of my daughter, Jenny. In the days that my mother prepared this, fresh mushrooms were not easily found, so she would use canned. Now I make this with fresh ingredients.

3 tablespoons vegetable oil
1 large onion, diced (about 2 cups)
4 carrots, diced
4 stalks celery, diced
1 cup butter
1 cup flour
2 cups milk
4 cups chicken broth
1 tablespoon dried herbs such as thyme, herbs de Provence, or parsley
1 tablespoon ground black pepper
2 tablespoons salt
3 tablespoons Worcestershire sauce
2 bay leaves
1 pound fresh mushrooms, sliced
8 ounces frozen peas, defrosted
6 cups diced cooked turkey
2 (4-ounce) jars canned diced pimentos, drained
Salt and pepper to taste
Optional garnish: Additional chopped pimentos or chopped flat leaf parsley

In a large Dutch oven, heat oil over medium-low heat and sauté onions until translucent, about 5 minutes. Add carrots and celery; cook over medium heat for 10 minutes. Remove from pan and set aside.

In same pan on medium-low heat, combine butter and flour, stirring constantly. Gradually add milk and chicken broth, simmering over medium heat until thickened.

Add herbs, pepper, salt, Worcestershire sauce, and bay leaves. Return cooked onions, carrots, and celery to pot with mushrooms, peas, turkey, and pimentos. Simmer 10 minutes.

Taste and add salt and pepper if needed. If mixture is too thick, add additional milk or chicken broth until it is the consistency of a nice gravy. Enjoy hot.

Dressing for Turkey

Serves 10 plus

This was the dressing we grew up with. When it was cooked in the turkey, it was called stuffing. More often, it was cooked outside of the bird for two reasons—and should be called a dressing. First, the turkey cooks faster unstuffed. Second, only a small amount of stuffing can fit in the bird. When you are cooking for a crowd, you'll want a larger quantity of dressing that you can eat with gravy and cranberry sauce. I'm getting hungry.

1 pound pork sausage, regular or sage-flavored
1 large onion, chopped
5 stalks celery, chopped
2 tablespoons ground sage (omit if sausage is sage-flavored)
1 teaspoon salt
1 teaspoon pepper
½ cup chopped parsley, American curly leaf or flat leaf
12 slices bread, left out to dry for 4 hours and torn into ¾-inch pieces
Optional: Chicken broth

In a large skillet over medium heat, cook sausage until browned, 10 to 15 minutes. Add onions and celery; cook until vegetables are tender, about 15 minutes.

Add sage (if using), salt, pepper, and parsley; turn off heat. Cool 10 minutes and add bread. Thoroughly mix. Mixture can be refrigerated at this point, so this is good to do the day before you roast the turkey.

Heat oven to 350°F. Put dressing in a covered casserole dish and bake 1 hour. After 30 minutes, check dressing. For a more moist dressing, add chicken broth. For a crusty top, remove cover and continue baking for 15 minutes.

Serve hot or at room temperature.

Soft white bread was the norm back in the day. We didn't have the choices that are available now.

Beef and Lamb

In my mother's day, most families were trying to expand their budgets. Many recipes of the time combined economical ground beef with inexpensive macaroni. Some of these dishes became our favorites, such as the More Casserole, so named because you will ask for "more," and Slumgullion, a funny-sounding name for another filling casserole. Both are economical, easy to prepare, and can feed a large family.

It would be easy to update these dishes. For example, in the past, cheese meant cottage, cheddar, or American, not the myriad choices you'll find in today's markets. Substitute manchego, blue cheese, smoked gouda, Grana Padano, or any combination of cheeses.

Meats roasted in the oven were also popular, as an inexpensive cut, cooked long and slow, could be transformed into a fabulous meal. Start it, walk away, and start tackling the long list of chores around the house. A few hours later, you would return to a tender meat with sauce. Lamb shanks, oxtail stew, leg of lamb, or pot roast were commonly cooked this way.

As children, we loved the gravy and didn't see how my mother was stretching to feed a large family. The food memories we have are so vivid, aren't they?

Twist Peppers and Beef

Serves 4 to 6

The twist peppers found in Korean markets are surprising. Some are mild and some are so hot they will make you cry. Sweet or hot, their flavors are quite delicious. My mother enjoyed this dish made by her friend Sue Youth and told me about it. I have tried to recreate her recipe.

2 tablespoons sesame oil
2 pounds beef chuck, cut into
  1-inch slices
1 cup soy sauce

1 cup sugar
½ cup water
1 pound twist peppers, stems
  removed

In a Dutch oven on medium-high, add sesame oil and beef slices; stir until meat has been seared. Reduce heat to medium-low; add soy sauce, sugar, and water. Cook 30 minutes, until beef is tender.

Add twist peppers whole and continue to cook until tender, about 10 minutes. Serve with hot steamed rice.

Note: A similar pepper is shishito pepper, sold in Japanese markets.

Teriyaki Steak or Barbecue Sticks

Serves 6 to 8

Use this marinade for steak or for meat on skewers—the type we used to order at the many saimin shops throughout Hawai'i.

2 pounds rib-eye, sirloin or flank steak
2 tablespoons oil
¼ cup green onions

Marinade:
½ cup soy sauce
¼ cup sugar
2 ounces liquor, whiskey, bourbon or what you have in the cupboard
1-inch piece ginger, thinly sliced or pounded
1 large clove garlic, minced

In a bowl or tray that will hold all the meat, combine marinade ingredients. Add beef and marinate, covered and refrigerated, for 2 hours.

In a cast-iron skillet on high, heat oil, then sear the meat for a few minutes on each side. Alternatively, cook the beef over a grill. Rest the meat for at least 5 minutes, then slice across the grain.

For Barbecue Sticks, also called Meat Sticks:
Cut the meat into thin strips and soak at least an hour in the marinade. Soak wooden skewers in water at least 30 minutes. Skewer meat on the sticks, threading them in and out. You will probably use 2 or 3 pieces per stick. Grill or broil the meat until done, just a few minutes on each side.

Beef Stroganoff

Serves 4 to 6

In the '60s, we considered this dish fancy food. My mother would make it for company. It seemed special because she would serve it over buttered egg noodles instead of our usual steamed white rice, and the cream sauce is comforting. Sometimes, when there was leftover roast beef, she would make it just for the family.

2 tablespoons oil
1 pound roast beef, tenderloin or flank steak, cut into 1-inch by 2-inch strips
½ pound fresh sliced button or cremini mushrooms (about 2½ cups)
½ cup butter
¼ cup flour

1 cup beef broth
1 tablespoon Worcestershire sauce
2 teaspoons salt
1 teaspoon pepper
½ cup sour cream
12 ounces egg noodles, or pasta of your choice, cooked to package directions
Minced parsley, for garnish

In a large skillet or Dutch oven, heat oil on medium heat and add beef. Stir 3 to 4 minutes. Add mushrooms and cook 3 to 4 minutes, until softened.

Remove meat and mushrooms; set aside. Add butter to the liquid in the skillet and melt over medium heat. Add flour, stirring constantly until mixture is thickened.

Add beef broth, Worcestershire sauce, salt and pepper and stir to make a gravy. Add sour cream, then return beef and mushrooms to skillet. Continue cooking on medium-low or low heat until beef and mushrooms are completely cooked. Do not let boil, as the sour cream could separate.

Serve warm over cooked noodles with a garnish of minced parsley.

Beef Stew

Serves 6 to 8

When I was in intermediate school (now they call it middle school), my sister and I ate dinner at a friend's home. We were shocked that they served beef stew with sliced bread and there was no rice to be found. Our friend's mother hailed from the mainland and liked bread with her stew. This staple dinner is actually good with poi, pasta, rice, or bread.

3 tablespoons vegetable oil
2 pounds chuck roast, cut into
   1-inch cubes
1 teaspoon kosher salt
1 teaspoon freshly ground black
   pepper
3 onions, wedged
4 sticks celery, cut into ½-inch
   pieces
1½ teaspoons dried herbs such
   as rosemary, thyme or herbs de
   Provence
1 (28-ounce) can of Italian plum
   tomatoes or San Marzano
   tomatoes
2 cups homemade chicken stock,
   or substitute low-sodium
   prepared chicken stock

2 cups red wine
5 cloves garlic, peeled and
   smashed
3 large carrots, peeled and cut
   into 1-inch chunks
Optional: 3 parsnips, peeled and
   cut into 1-inch chunks
3 russet potatoes, peeled and cut
   into 2-inch chunks
½ head of cabbage, cut into
   2-inch pieces
Salt and pepper to taste
Optional: 1 tablespoon flour
   mixed with two tablespoons
   cold water
Chopped flat leaf parsley, minced,
   for garnish

In a large Dutch oven, heat oil, then brown beef on medium-high for about 5 minutes, until all sides are seared. Sprinkle with salt and pepper. Add onions, celery, and dried herbs; cook over medium heat another 5 minutes, stirring often until onions are half-cooked.

Use your hands to break tomatoes into small pieces; add with their liquid to pot. Add chicken stock, wine, garlic, and enough water to cover. Simmer 2 hours on medium heat with cover slightly ajar.

(continued on the next page)

Add carrots (and parsnips if using) with more water to cover all the vegetables. Continue cooking on medium-low 30 more minutes. Beef should be tender. If not, cook longer.

Add potatoes and simmer until soft, about 30 minutes more. Skim oil. Five minutes before serving, add cabbage and salt and pepper. The potatoes will thicken the gravy, but if you like it thicker, stir in a slurry (flour and water mixed until smooth). Simmer until mixture thickens, about 5 minutes on medium heat.

Garnish with chopped flat leaf parsley. Serve hot with bread, rice, polenta, or poi. This is even better the next day!

Spinach Lasagna

Serves 8 to 10

Jean Grimes would make this recipe for her son, my brother-in-law, Tom Grimes, and his siblings—Bud, Susan, Laurel, and Joe.

2 pounds ground beef, 80 to 90 percent lean
1 tablespoon chopped parsley
Handful fresh oregano or mixture of oregano and basil
2 teaspoons salt
2 (10-ounce) packages chopped spinach, blanched and drained
3 eggs, beaten
1 quart bottled spaghetti sauce
Lasagna noodles, cooked according to package directions
16 ounces mozzarella cheese, roughly grated

In a saucepan, brown beef. Add herbs and salt; set aside.

Squeeze water from spinach and mix with eggs. Set aside.

Preheat oven to 325°F. In a 9 x 13-inch pan, ladle enough spaghetti sauce to thinly cover bottom. Top with three cooked lasagna noodles. Top with ⅓ of spinach mixture, then ⅓ of the beef and ⅓ of the cheese. Repeat these layers twice, ending with sauce on top.

Cover with foil and bake 1 hour. Remove from oven and test the center. If it is not hot, bake another 30 minutes.

Remove from oven and let rest 20 minutes. Cut and serve.

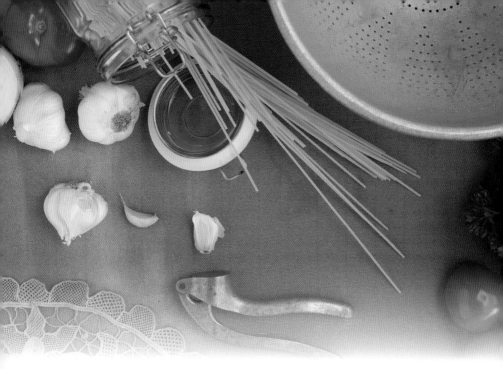

Honeymoon Spaghetti

Serves 4 to 6

Why the name honeymoon spaghetti? It's a very easy and quick recipe, so one supposes you can do other things on your honeymoon! The spaghetti noodles are broken into small pieces and cooked in the sauce, not in a separate pot. My sister often cooked a dish similar to this one when we were in high school and it was her turn to make a fast family dinner.

1 pound ground beef, 80 to 90 percent lean
2 tablespoons vegetable oil
⅓ cup finely chopped onion
1 (28-ounce) can stewed tomatoes and juices, broken up or chopped

½ cup ketchup
½ teaspoon salt
¼ teaspoon pepper
1 tablespoon Worcestershire sauce
1 tablespoon brown sugar
6 ounces spaghetti, broken into 1-inch pieces

In a large saucepan or skillet, brown beef in oil. Skim fat. Add the rest of the ingredients except the spaghetti noodles; simmer on medium low for 30 minutes.

Add spaghetti and cook until tender, about 15 minutes. Enjoy hot.

Hamburger Steak and Gravy

Makes 6 patties

Hamburger is popular with children, served either with gravy or on hamburger buns with lettuce, tomato, and onions. The basic burger in this recipe can be used either way.

1 pound ground beef, 80 percent lean recommended
¼ cup chopped onion
¼ cup whole milk
¼ cup breadcrumbs
1 teaspoon salt
½ teaspoon pepper
1 egg
2 teaspoons Worcestershire sauce
3 tablespoons oil

Gravy:
2 tablespoons flour
1 (14.5-ounce) can beef broth
Salt and pepper to taste
Optional: ½ to 1 cup sliced mushrooms

In a bowl, combine beef, onion, milk, breadcrumbs, salt, pepper, and egg. Form 6 patties. In a skillet, heat oil over medium and fry patties until done, about 5 minutes on each side.

To make gravy: In the same skillet, heat the hamburger drippings and stir in flour until well-blended. Gradually stir in beef broth and bring to a boil. Stir in salt and pepper. If using, add mushrooms and simmer until cooked, about 5 minutes. Pour gravy over hamburger steaks.

We always seemed to have enough food, even when our friends came over unannounced. My mother would cook more rice or pasta, add more cabbage, or open cans of pork and beans or Vienna sausages. Somehow the meals managed to S-T-R-E-T-C-H.

More Casserole

We would ask my mother to make MORE, a satisfying casserole that seems to include the kitchen sink. Adapt it to whatever ingredients your family likes.

- 12 ounces shell pasta or elbow macaroni
- 2 cups frozen peas, defrosted
- 1 pound ground beef, 80 to 90 percent lean
- 3 onions, chopped
- 1 tablespoon dry hot mustard
- 1 (4-ounce) bottle sliced pimentos, drained
- 1 (6-ounce) can pitted sliced black olives, drained
- 1 (10.5-ounce) can tomato soup
- 1 (14.75-ounce) can creamed corn
- 1 tablespoon Worcestershire sauce
- 1 tablespoon paprika, any type
- 1 teaspoon ground black pepper
- 1 teaspoon garlic salt
- 1 cup grated cheddar cheese

Boil pasta 3 minutes, or according to package directions. Place peas in a colander; empty pasta pot over peas. Cool with cold water, drain; set aside.

In a large skillet or Dutch oven, brown beef and onions over medium heat until meat is cooked and onions are translucent, about 10 minutes.

Preheat oven to 325°F. In a 9 x 13-inch (or larger) baking pan or casserole dish, add pasta, beef mixture, and the rest of the ingredients, except cheese. Mix thoroughly. Top with cheese and bake uncovered for 40 minutes. Your dinner guests will ask for MORE.

Slumgullion

Serves 10 to 12

This is a satisfying meal for a large family. Basically, a hamburger, macaroni and cheese dish, it sneaks in corn, carrots, and peas to add a bit of nutrition. The funny name derives from old English slang for slime (slum) and mud (gullion). There are many versions of this dish, all inexpensive. Call it a casserole or a stew, our family ate this often and enjoyed it.

- 1 cup elbow or salad (short) macaroni
- 1 pound ground beef, 80 to 90 percent lean
- 1 tablespoon oil
- 1 large onion, chopped (about 2 cups)
- 1 (14.5-ounce) can diced tomatoes
- 1 (15-ounce) can tomato sauce

- 2 cups frozen peas and carrots, defrosted
- 2 teaspoons salt or garlic salt
- 2 teaspoons pepper
- 1 teaspoon paprika
- 3 large cloves garlic, minced
- 1¾ cup frozen, defrosted, or canned corn, drained
- 1 cup grated cheddar cheese

Bring a pot of water to boil. Add macaroni and cook according to package instructions, about 5 minutes.

While pasta is cooking, in a large skillet, brown beef in oil over medium-high heat, stirring often, about 10 minutes. Add onions and cook until translucent, about 10 minutes. Add tomatoes, tomato sauce, peas and carrots; cook 5 more minutes, until carrots are tender and no longer crunchy.

Add salt, pepper, paprika, garlic, and corn. Cook 5 more minutes. Mix in cheddar cheese and drained macaroni. Serve immediately with hot sauce on the side.

Baked Oxtail Stew

Serves 8 to 10

Don't slave over a stove. Enjoy oxtails after they've cooked until tender in the oven.

3 pounds oxtails
2 large onions, chopped
6 cloves garlic, chopped
1 (28-ounce) can stewed tomatoes
6 tablespoons soy sauce
6 tablespoons Worcestershire sauce
1 heaping tablespoon brown sugar

1-inch piece ginger, peeled and smashed
2 teaspoons pepper
2 carrots, peeled and cut into 1-inch pieces
2 stalks celery, cut into 1-inch pieces
2 salad potatoes, cut into 1-inch pieces
Beef broth as needed

Preheat oven to 325°F. In a large Dutch oven, combine oxtails with onions, garlic, tomatoes, soy sauce, Worcestershire sauce, brown sugar, ginger and pepper. Cover and place in an oven 2 hours and 15 minutes. Test for tenderness.

Reduce heat to 300°F and add carrots, celery, and potatoes. If more cooking liquid is needed, add beef broth. Continue cooking 45 more minutes. Skim oil and serve hot.

Pūlehu Ribs

When we camped on the beach near Kualoa, this was a favorite meal, cooked over a hot grill. Beef marinates much quicker than chicken, so all you need is to soak it for an hour and the taste is delicious.

2 pounds (about 4) beef back ribs
Chopped green onions and
**   sesame seeds, for garnish**

Salt rub:
1 large clove garlic
2 Hawaiian chili peppers
2 teaspoons Hawaiian salt
1 tablespoon pepper

To make rub: On a cutting board, mince together garlic and chili pepper. Add salt and pepper. Mix well.

Remove silver skin from back of ribs and cut into individual ribs. Rub salt rub over both sides of ribs and refrigerate for 1 hour.

Place ribs curved side down on a foil-lined pan. Broil on high 10 minutes. Flip ribs and continue broiling 5 more minutes. Or grill on a hot barbecue.

Garnish with green onions and/or sesame seeds. Enjoy hot.

My daughter Jenny and niece Sara loved my mother's pronunciation of "chili pepper." They'd ask her question after question about how she made poke or pulehu beef ribs, or spaghetti, just so they could hear her say, "chilah peppah."

Pot Roast

Serves 8 to 10

This is a great comfort dish that uses an inexpensive cut of beef and feeds many as it contains a large amount of vegetables and gravy. It is similar to a stew, but does not contain tomatoes. My mother says the key is slicing the cooked meat first in chunks and then sideways, against the grain, which makes it tender.

1 (4 to 4½-pound) chuck roast
3 tablespoons oil
2 cups sliced onions
2 garlic cloves, minced
2 bay leaves
1 teaspoon dried thyme
1 (14.5-ounce) can beef broth
1 tablespoon salt
1 tablespoon pepper

2 large carrots, peeled and cut into 2-inch pieces
2 stalks celery, cut into 2-inch pieces
8 red potatoes, washed and cut in half
2 tablespoons flour
4 tablespoons cold water

In a large skillet or Dutch oven, brown meat in oil over high heat. Add onions, garlic, bay leaves, thyme, beef broth, salt, and pepper. Cover and simmer about 3 hours.

Add carrots, celery, and potatoes; cook on medium heat until both meat and vegetables are tender, 25 to 30 minutes. Add water as needed.

In a small bowl, mix flour and water until dissolved. Pour into skillet and stir until a gravy forms, about 5 minutes. Season with salt and pepper.

Remove meat and cut it in chunks against the grain. Return meat to pot and serve hot.

Oven Lamb Shank Stew

Serves 4

This recipe is easily doubled for a party. It's good to make the day before, then warm up for your guests.

2 tablespoons oil
4 lamb shanks
2 teaspoons salt
1 tablespoon black pepper
4 onions, cut in wedges
4 stalks celery, cut into thirds
4 carrots, peeled and cut into 2-inch pieces
4 parsnips, peeled and cut into 2-inch pieces, optional
Optional: 8 ounces whole button or cremini (baby Portobello) mushrooms
1 cup dry red wine

⅔ cup ketchup
3 tablespoons freshly squeezed lemon juice
4 cloves garlic, peeled and smashed
1 teaspoon dried oregano, or fresh thyme or rosemary
3 bay leaves
Optional: 2 tablespoons flour, cornstarch or mochiko (rice flour)
Garnish: Minced flat leaf parsley or gremolata

Preheat oven to 400°F. In a cast-iron skillet, heat oil and brown each shank. Sprinkle each with salt and pepper. Place in a large casserole dish or roasting pan. Add onions, celery, carrots, plus parsnips and mushrooms (if using). Stir in wine, ketchup, lemon juice, garlic, oregano, and bay leaves into casserole.

Cover with foil and bake 2 hours, then test whether meat is tender. If you would like a thicker sauce, mix flour or cornstarch with ¼ cup room-temperature water thoroughly and add to dish. Or stir mochiko directly into sauce. Stir over medium heat until sauce is thickened, about 10 minutes.

Garnish with minced flat leaf parsley. Enjoy this stew hot with pasta or rice.

Note: Gremolata is an Italian condiment that goes with rich meat dishes such as this one or veal shanks (osso buco). It is a mixture of finely minced garlic, flat leaf parsley, and lemon or orange zest, used to garnish a dish.

Roasted Leg of Lamb

Serves 8

I find that many people do not appreciate the taste of lamb. Fortunately, my mother and father enjoyed lamb and would cook shanks (see page 65) and this delicious garlic and rosemary-scented leg of lamb. Back then, it always was sold with the bone. Now it is easily found without the bone, and that makes it easy to roast and to carve.

1 (6- to 8-pound) leg of lamb, boneless	3 tablespoons dried rosemary or fresh rosemary sprigs
6 large cloves of garlic, each sliced into 4 pieces	1 teaspoon oregano
¼ cup olive oil	1 tablespoon salt
	2 teaspoons pepper

Preheat oven to 325°F on the roast setting if you have that. If not, use the bake setting. Line a roasting pan with foil.

Rinse lamb to remove any blood. Pat dry. With a sharp knife, make holes in the meat. In each hole, insert a piece of garlic. Place meat in roasting pan and cover completely with oil. Sprinkle with rosemary, oregano, salt, and pepper.

Roast about 3 hours, to an internal temperature of 120°F for rare. If the roast is large, it could take an additional hour. Test with an instant read thermometer. Cover with foil and let rest at least 15 minutes before carving. Serve with mango chutney or mint jelly.

Alternatively, butterfly the lamb and let it marinate in ingredients at least 6 hours. Grill or cook in a kamado (now called the "Green Egg") OR grill on a high fire for 20 to 30 minutes for rare.

Our family about 1965. (L-R) Barry, mother Lorna, Charlene, me, Joanne, and my dad Richard Lo carrying Russell.

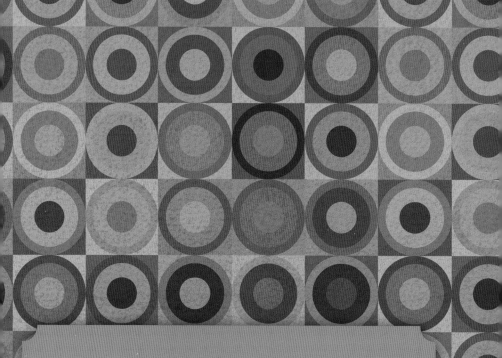

Pork

Pork was one of my father's favorite foods. I can still picture him with a huge bowl of pork bones that had been boiled for soup. He enjoyed seeking out the slivers of meat hidden on the bones, dipping them in soy sauce.

Pork is the foundation of so many of our home-style comfort foods. My mother's recipe for baked ham is a case in point. Every time she made it, someone asked for her recipe as it is so moist and flavorful. It left little room for improvement until a cousin through marriage shared his mother's recipe for a raisin sauce. It transforms ham to another level and has become a permanent pairing for our family.

Other friends have added to our repertoire of pork dishes. Taren Taguchi, was generous in sharing her kobumaki recipe with my mother, and it became one of her favorites. The tasty strips of pork and gobo are simmered in a soy sauce mixture until tender. It is an okazuya (Japanese delicatessen) specialty, but Taren's is better!

Enjoy all the recipes for this favorite protein of Chinese and Okinawans.

Kobumaki (or Konbu Maki)

Kelp-Wrapped Pork and Burdock Rolls

Makes about 26

Burdock is considered a weed in some parts of the mainland, but in Hawai'i and Japan, its distinctive taste and woody texture are treasured. This tasty and savory Japanese dish is the perfect combination of fatty pork, burdock, and nutritious kelp seaweed simmered in a traditional braising liquid of soy sauce and sugar. The bundles look like presents with their double-knotted ties of white dried gourd (kampyo). You may just end up eating any imperfect ones yourself.

1 large gobo (burdock), peeled and cut into 2½-inch lengths, then quartered lengthwise
1 (1-ounce) package konbu (kelp)
1 pound boneless pork butt or pork shoulder, cut into 2 x ½-inch strips

1 (0.7-ounce) bag kampyo (dried gourd strips), soaked in water
1 cup soy sauce
1 cup sugar
2-inch ginger, sliced and crushed
2 garlic cloves, crushed
2 cups water

Soak gobo in water for at least 30 minutes. Wash konbu and cut into 3-inch lengths; soak in water 15 minutes.

Place a piece of gobo and pork on one end of a piece of konbu. Roll tightly, then use a length of kampyo to tie up the bundle in the middle, using a double knot. Repeat until all the ingredients are used.

Put the rolls in a saucepan with a cover with any extra pork or gobo. Cover with soy sauce, sugar, ginger, garlic, and water. Cover and simmer until tender, about 1 hour. For fancy occasions, you can trim the ends of the rolls so they are uniform.

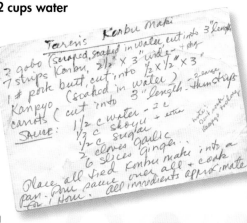

Baked Ham

Serves 20 to 30

When I bake a ham using my mother's method, people ask for the recipe, which is very easy. They cannot believe how juicy and tasty ham can be when it's not overcooked. My mother prefers to buy the Farmer John brand and slice it herself. Allow about ½ pound per person, not counting the bone. She says you can use the pre-sliced variety, but need to be even more careful not to overbake it. Ever the pragmatist, she says you can use any type of leftover jam or jelly such as guava or liliko'i for the glaze, but orange marmalade is especially good. I would use lighter colors such as red, orange, or yellow jams, not grape or blueberry.

- 1 whole ham, bone-in (10 to 18 pounds)
- 1 tablespoon dry hot mustard, such as Coleman's
- ½ cup brown sugar
- 2 teaspoons ground cloves
- ½ cup jam, jelly or marmalade
- 1 (8-ounce) can crushed pineapple in pineapple juice, optional

Preheat oven to 325°F.

Slice ham into pieces about 3 x 3 x ½ inches. They do not need to be exact. Layer them in a 9 x 13-inch pan or a large casserole. You will not need a cover. Bake until ham is heated through, 30 to 60 minutes, depending on how cold the ham is, how many layers you have, and how you stack them.

Save the bone for another use, such as Portuguese bean, split pea, or lentil soup, or Chinese rice gruel (jook).

In a bowl, mix mustard powder, brown sugar, cloves, and jelly. Mix in pineapples and juice, if using.

Spread jelly mixture over the warmed ham pieces; broil until golden. Watch carefully as this will take only a few minutes.

Raisin Sauce for Ham

Enough sauce for a 10 to 18-pound ham

Auntie Yuki Hirata was a top-notch cook for husband Timmy Hirata's friends while he was McKinley High School's principal and, later, the Department of Education's superintendent. One of her memorable offerings was a raisin sauce that took a ham from good to great. It can be served on the side in a gravy boat. You'll never go back to serving a naked ham.

¾ cup raisins
¾ cup brown sugar
1 tablespoon butter
1 tablespoon vinegar
1 tablespoon lemon juice

5 whole cloves or dash of ground
  cloves
1 teaspoon cornstarch
⅛ teaspoon paprika
Dash Worcestershire sauce
1 cup water
Drippings from baked ham

In a pot combine all ingredients except the drippings. Simmer uncovered 2 to 3 hours over the lowest heat. Add drippings from your baked ham in the last 5 minutes of simmering. The sauce will be thick like a gravy. Serve alongside ham.

An old recipe called for meat to be marinated in Oly. Do you know what that is? Olympia Beer, originally made in Tumwater, Wash.

Oven Kālua Pig

Serves 8 to 10

This is an easy recipe, and pork butt (also called shoulder) is one of the least expensive meats in the market.

4 to 5 pounds pork butt or pork shoulder
1 tablespoon liquid smoke

1 tablespoon Kitchen Bouquet
2 tablespoons Hawaiian rock salt
2 ti leaves, cleaned

Preheat oven to 350°F.

Rub pork with liquid smoke and Kitchen Bouquet. Place fat side down in a large casserole or baking pan. Sprinkle with salt and cover with ti leaves, then foil. Roast 1 hour. Halfway through, uncover, turn meat over, cover again and resume cooking.

Let stand 15 minutes covered, then discard ti leaves and cut or shred the meat. Add more salt to taste if needed.

Sausage Potatoes and Onions

Serves 4 to 6

This easy and hearty dish was often served in our house. It was dinner in one skillet. If you only have a few sausages, you can stretch this to feed a large family by adding more potatoes. It's an economical dish and easily pulled together if you have sausages in the freezer and onions and potatoes in your pantry.

6 assorted sausage links, 2 to 3 varieties such as Italian, garlic, frankfurters
2 tablespoons vegetable oil
1 large onion, sliced

3 large Yukon gold potatoes, unpeeled and sliced into rounds
Black pepper to taste
Optional garnish: Minced parsley

In a large skillet on medium heat, brown sausage links in oil about 5 minutes. Stir sausages so they are browned on all sides. Using a fork, prick sausage casings and add onions. Cover and reduce heat to medium-low. Stir occasionally for 3 minutes.

Remove sausages and cut them diagonally, then return to pan. Add potatoes, cover, and stir every few minutes until tender, about 10 minutes. Add pepper. Garnish with parsley and serve hot or at room temperature, with mustard on the side.

Variations:
- Add 1 cup of drained sauerkraut when adding the potatoes.
- Omit oil and add ½ cup of beer at the beginning.
- Use whole fingerling potatoes for a more elegant look.

Pork Chops with Onion Gravy

Serves 4 to 6

My father loved to eat this for dinner, always seeking out the slices with the bones. My mother says you cannot use an expensive cut of pork chops, you must buy the cheaper, bony, fattier cuts. Surprisingly for that era, the sauce did not include a condensed cream soup. The gravy becomes tasty from the simmered onions and herbs.

4 bone-in pork chops
2 tablespoons oil
3 onions, sliced
2 cloves garlic, minced
1 tablespoon Worcestershire sauce
2 teaspoons salt
1 teaspoon pepper

1 teaspoon dried thyme, Italian seasoning, or herbs de Provence
½ cup water
Optional: 8 ounces fresh sliced mushrooms or canned mushrooms, drained
1 tablespoon cornstarch, dissolved in 2 tablespoons cold water

Wash pork chops to remove any bone fragments. Pat dry with paper towels.

In a large skillet, heat oil on medium-high and brown the pork chops in batches, about 4 minutes on each side. Remove from skillet to a cutting board.

Reduce heat to medium and add onions to skillet. Cook until translucent, then add garlic, Worcestershire sauce, salt, pepper, and thyme.

Cut pork chops into strips and return to skillet. Add water. Cover and cook until pork chops are tender, about 30 minutes. Add mushrooms, if using. Test pork for doneness. Skim fat.

Mix cornstarch slurry and add to liquid in skillet. Stir until thickened and a gravy is formed. Enjoy hot and serve over noodles or rice.

Seafood and Fish

It would be difficult to find someone of my generation who hasn't eaten tuna casserole. It was a hot meal that could feed many mouths using the inexpensive ingredients of canned tuna, canned peas, noodles, and cream of mushroom soup. It was considered fancy with a topping of crushed potato chips. Simple canned salmon was also popular, combined with bitter watercress and tofu as a refreshing salad.

Fresh fish from our island waters also made its way to our table. Some of my favorites: aku bones marinated and coated with cornstarch, then fried; 'ahi belly broiled and made even more 'ono (delicious) with a Japanese grated daikon sauce; and, of course, 'ahi poke.

Other types of seafood were considered fancy food—shrimp, for example. Shrimp Canlis from the Canlis restaurant in Waikīkī, the epitome of fine food and white tablecloths, was a classic. At home, shrimp curry was considered exotic party food, served with a side of rice and many condiments showcased in monkey pod bowls.

What could be classier?

ʻAhi Poke

Serves 4 to 6 as an appetizer

At our family parties, my mother would make a delicious ʻahi poke. She wouldn't measure. She would just casually toss the ingredients together at the last minute and everyone would enjoy it. In a few minutes, it would be gone. This recipe attempts to recreate the fresh taste of her raw tuna mix with simple ingredients.

1 pound sashimi-grade ʻahi, cut in ½-inch cubes
1 teaspoon sesame oil
½ teaspoon rock salt
½ teaspoon finely grated ginger
½ teaspoon dried chili flakes or minced Hawaiian chili pepper
3 tablespoons chopped green onions
½ onion (about 1 cup) thinly sliced
1 teaspoon soy sauce
Optional: ¼ cup chopped fresh ogo (seaweed)

Mix fish with sesame oil, then add remaining ingredients. Serve immediately.

Note: Should you be so lucky to have any leftover poke, quickly pan-fry it to make a tasty, slightly cooked version of the dish.

There are two main ways of slicing onions. Cutting from the top to the root results in a stronger slice that will stay crunchy when raw and remain intact longer when cooked. When you cut an onion against the grain, it will turn to mush faster. Choose your cut based on the onion texture you want in your dish.

Mahimahi with Tartar Sauce

Serves 4

This was a favorite dish of ours, so my mother made it often. It tasted much better than what was served in restaurants. Usually she would use frozen fish, which was easier to get than freshly caught in those days. Her trick was to soak the fish in milk for at least an hour, and somehow that soaking made it taste very fresh.

1½ pounds fresh or frozen mahimahi, skin removed
1 cup milk
1 teaspoon salt
1 teaspoon pepper
2 tablespoons butter
2 tablespoons olive oil

Optional: 1 tablespoon capers
Garnish: 1 tablespoon minced flat leaf parsley
1 lemon cut into wedges
Tartar Sauce, to taste (recipe follows)

Cut fish into sections, removing the middle part with the bones and darker bloodline. Soak fish in milk in the refrigerator at least an hour. Discard milk.

Dry on paper towels and season with salt and pepper. In a saucepan, melt butter over medium-low heat. Add olive oil and capers, if using. Place fish in pan and cook until done, about 4 minutes per side.

Plate immediately, garnish with parsley, and serve with a wedge of lemon and Tartar Sauce.

Tartar Sauce

½ cup mayonnaise (Best Foods preferred)
½ onion (about 1 cup), chopped

2 tablespoons sweet pickle relish
1 tablespoon lemon juice

Mix ingredients. Cover with plastic wrap and chill until ready to use.

Salmon Tofu Watercress Salad

Serves 4 to 6

My mother learned this recipe from her relative, Myrna Chun-Hoon. We found it to be very refreshing. You can add bean sprouts for even more crunch.

1½ (20-ounce) blocks firm tofu, drained
1 medium sweet onion, chopped or thinly sliced
1 tomato, diced
1 (7.5-ounce) can salmon
1 bunch (about 6 cups) watercress, rinsed and cut into 1-inch lengths
Optional: Toasted sesame seeds for garnish

Dressing:
¼ cup sesame oil
2 cloves garlic, minced
½ cup soy sauce
½ cup green onion, chopped

Drain tofu, cut it into ½-inch cubes. Place into a large rimmed platter or bowl. Add onions, tomatoes, salmon, and watercress.

To make dressing: In a saucepan, heat oil and add garlic. Turn off heat. Add soy sauce and green onions. Pour over vegetables and tofu. Serve immediately or refrigerate. Garnish just before serving with sesame seeds, if desired.

Tuna Casserole

Serves 6 to 8

Is there anyone in Hawai'i who hasn't eaten tuna casserole? This is an all-American comfort food pulled together with the Hawai'i favorite—cream of mushroom soup. In other parts of the country, cream of celery or cream of chicken might be used, but not here. This dish is easily made ahead without the potato chip topping, refrigerated, then baked later with the topping.

12 ounces egg noodles or any shaped pasta
2 teaspoons salt
2 (10.5-ounce) cans condensed cream of mushroom soup
2 (5-ounce) cans tuna, in oil preferred, drained
1 cup grated cheddar cheese
½ onion, finely chopped
1 cup frozen peas, defrosted
1 teaspoon pepper
1 teaspoon cayenne pepper
1 cup potato chips, crushed

Cook egg noodles in salted water to al dente, according to package instructions. Drain; set aside.

Preheat oven to 350°F. Mix noodles with soup, tuna, cheese, onion, peas, and pepper; place in a large casserole or baking pan. Sprinkle with cayenne pepper, then the potato chips. Bake 30 minutes. Serve hot or at room temperature.

'Ahi Belly

Serves 2 to 3 depending on the size of the fish.

1 'ahi belly fillet

1 teaspoon Hawaiian rock salt

Remove skin if still on, but keep the cartilage that holds the fish together. Place on a pan covered in foil, cartilage side down. Sprinkle with salt. Broil on high 5 to 10 minutes, until top is slightly brown and fish is cooked. Be careful not to overcook, as 'ahi is good rare.

Serve with lemon wedges and/or Chiri Sauce (see recipe below).

Chiri Sauce for Fish

Makes about 1 cup

This Japanese-style sauce was served with broiled 'ahi belly at the now-closed Wisteria Restaurant. The grated daikon sauce is good with any fish or fresh or fried tofu.

1½ cups grated daikon (white radish)
3 tablespoons soy sauce
2 tablespoons mirin

1 teaspoon freshly squeezed lemon juice, substitute yuzu or lime citrus
Optional: 1 teaspoon sake
Garnish: Chopped green onions
Optional: Togarashi shichimi powder

Drain daikon. Mix with soy sauce, mirin, and lemon juice. Add sake if desired. Chill at least 1 hour for flavors to merge.

Top with green onions and serve with fish. If you like it spicy, add the Japanese chili powder called togarashi shichimi.

Note: Grated daikon emits lots of liquid. I prefer to drain the daikon before mixing it with soy sauce, mirin, and lemon juice to create a thicker sauce. But you may prefer sauce with more liquid.

Fried Aku Bones

Serves 2 to 4

Aku bones are a quintessential home food, rarely served in restaurants. My mother would make a delicious main course from what used to be the throwaway parts of large fish by marinating the meat, then frying it. There isn't much meat but my mother feels strongly that too much meat on the bones takes away the pleasure of finding the thin shreds between the bones. Less meat also means a crispier treat. As the saying goes, "The closer to the bone, the sweeter the meat."

2 pounds bones of a large fish such as aku or sea bass
½ cup cornstarch
Oil for frying
2 cups sliced cabbage
Garnish: Chopped green onions

Marinade:
¼ cup soy sauce
3 tablespoons liquor, such as bourbon, whiskey or whatever you have in your pantry
1 teaspoon sugar
2 inches ginger, peeled and thinly sliced
3 cloves garlic, smashed
1 Hawaiian chili pepper, finely chopped

Select bones with barely any meat, or remove the meat and cook that separately. Cut bones into 3-inch pieces.

In a shallow pan, combine marinade ingredients. Taste and adjust seasonings. Marinate fish bones in refrigerator for 1 hour, turning bones after 30 minutes so both sides are seasoned.

Remove fish and dredge in cornstarch, coating both sides. Heat oil in a skillet on medium-high, then fry fish about 2 minutes on each side. Be careful not to overcook, as aku tends to be dry.

Spread cabbage on a platter. Top with fish and garnish with green onions. Serve with Chiri Sauce (page 83) if desired.

Another way: Fry the fish first, coated in cornstarch. Dip the fried fish in the marinade.

Shrimp Canlis

Serves 4 as an appetizer, more over pasta

It was always a treat to eat at the Canlis restaurant in Waikīkī. Canlis is no longer in Hawai'i, but is still winning restaurant awards at its Seattle location. This shrimp recipe is good as an appetizer or main dish.

1 tablespoon olive oil
1½ tablespoons butter
1 pound raw large shrimp, shelled
   and deveined
1 large clove garlic, minced
½ teaspoon Dijon mustard

¼ teaspoon salt
Dash pepper
¼ cup dry vermouth
Juice of half a lemon
2 tablespoons minced flat leaf
   parsley

Heat oil and butter in a large skillet over medium; add shrimp, and sauté 2 minutes. Reduce heat to low and add garlic, mustard, salt, and pepper; sauté 2 more minutes. Add vermouth and lemon juice, sauté another 2 minutes. Garnish with parsley.

Note: Turn this into a main dish by serving it over a pasta.

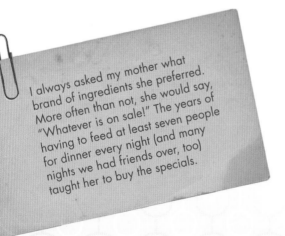

I always asked my mother what brand of ingredients she preferred. More often than not, she would say, "Whatever is on sale!" The years of having to feed at least seven people for dinner every night (and many nights we had friends over, too) taught her to buy the specials.

Shrimp Curry

Serves 8

I remember when this dish was served at every party and was considered exotic and fancy. The condiments were often presented in koa or monkey pod bowls, making it seem even more special.

2 bay leaves, crushed
2 large cloves garlic, crushed
½ lemon, sliced
1 tablespoon salt
6 cups of water
1½ pounds large shrimp, peeled, tails removed, and deveined
6 tablespoons butter, divided
¾ cup celery, finely chopped
3 tablespoons green bell pepper, finely chopped
2 teaspoons minced onion
½ cup flour

2 tablespoons curry powder
¼ teaspoon thyme
2½ cups half-and-half
½ teaspoon salt
¼ teaspoon white pepper
1 cup coconut milk

Condiments: Mango chutney, grated coconut, finely chopped peanuts, chopped crisp bacon, chopped hard boiled eggs, raisins, lemon wedges

In a small pot, combine bay leaves, garlic, lemon, and salt in water; bring to a boil. Add shrimp and reduce heat to simmer. Cook until shrimp are barely cooked; remove quickly. Cool. Set aside.

In a large saucepan, melt 3 tablespoons of the butter. Add celery, bell pepper, and onion. Cover and simmer until vegetables are tender, but do not let brown.

Add remaining butter with flour, curry powder, and thyme. Mix and gradually add half-and-half. Cook until thickened, stirring constantly. Add salt and pepper, more if desired. Reduce heat to lowest level; add coconut milk and return shrimp to pan. Serve immediately with rice and condiments.

Variation: Substitute boneless, skinless chicken thighs for the shrimp. Simmer them in oil before adding the curry sauce.

Side Dishes

When I was five years old, I started flying alone to San Jose, California, each summer to visit my aunt. Luckily, Auntie Lillian "Eio" Chu was the most talented cook and baker. She and her sons, JR and Clayton, cooked at their family's Manchu's Chinese Restaurant.

The restaurant was an adventure and a very popular place for Americanized Chinese food like egg foo yung, sweet-and-sour spareribs, fried rice, and chow mein.

Every dish Auntie Eio made was a standout. Try her Spicy Cranberry Relish and Onion Casserole.

In those days, Silicon Valley was filled with orchards, and I also remember getting peaches and apricots from the farmers. Good memories.

We tend to focus on the main dishes, but sides provide color, contrasting flavors, and some all-important ballast through the starch in rice and potato dishes.

In our house, rice was the staple side dish at almost every meal. We would cook it on the stove the old-fashioned way; no rice cooker was involved. When we cooked it at a higher temperature, we would get the much-desired slightly burned crusty rice at the bottom of the pot. When the rice was almost done, we'd add any leftover rice from the fridge to warm it up. No microwaves in those days.

Many of my family's favorites stole the show from the main dishes—from my mother's citrusy baked bananas to my cousin Pam Ching Leong's rice pilaf casserole to Auntie Helen's pineapple Jell-O mold.

Next time your main dish is something ordinary, the right side dish might be all you need to make the meal something spectacular.

Zucchini Juhn

Serves 6 to 8 as a side dish

This Korean recipe using easy-to-find zucchini squash makes a wonderful side dish. The timing and cut of the zucchini results in a tender texture. If you want the squash crispier, cut it thicker or cook it for less time. The simple dipping sauce is not spicy, so this battered vegetable is one of the few non-spicy side dishes at a Korean dinner.

**2 zucchinis, sliced ¼-inch
   at a diagonal
1 teaspoon salt
½ cup flour
2 eggs, beaten
¾ cup oil**

Sauce:
**¼ cup soy sauce
¼ cup white vinegar**

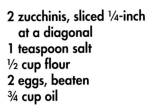

My mother was strict about not catering to our preferences. She served one main dish for dinner and if we said we didn't like it, she said "too bad." If we wanted to eat, we could make ourselves a sandwich. With five children to feed, she didn't want to make five different dishes.

Place zucchini slices in a bowl with salt; let sit 5 minutes. Pat dry.

Dredge zucchini in flour, then dip in beaten eggs.

Heat a large skillet with half of the oil. Fry battered zucchini squash in batches over medium heat for 2 to 3 minutes on each side. Drain on paper towels.

To make sauce: Mix soy sauce and vinegar. Serve Zucchini Juhn with sauce, hot or at room temperature.

Rice Pilaf

Serves 10 to 12

Don't let the simplicity of this recipe fool you. It makes a memorable side dish. The original recipe my mother used called for Uncle Ben's converted rice. I find that using long-grain rice turns out fine and is less expensive. The amount of fresh mushroom varies depending on your craving for the fungi. I like more.

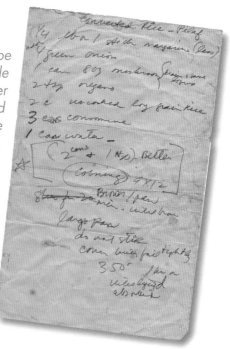

- 2 cups long-grain rice
- ¼ pound (1 stick) butter
- 4 green onions, chopped
- 6 to 12 ounces assorted fresh
  mushrooms, sliced
- 2 teaspoons oregano
- 2 (10.5-ounce) cans consommé
  soup
- 1¼ cans water

Preheat oven to 350°F. Wash and drain rice. Set aside.

In a skillet over medium heat, melt butter and brown rice for about 5 minutes. Stir in onions, mushrooms, and oregano. Pour into a 9 x 13-inch pan or casserole. Add soup and water. Cover with foil and bake 1 hour, until all liquid is dissolved and rice is cooked.

Serve hot or at room temperature.

Baked Bananas

Serves 6

This recipe is a great way to use extra bananas. It is so tasty, you will make it over and over again. Serve this with pork chops or roast pork or for dessert with a scoop of vanilla ice cream. Yum.

6 tablespoons butter
½ cup brown sugar
¼ cup orange juice
Juice of half a lemon

6 ripe but firm bananas, sliced lengthwise
¼ teaspoon cinnamon
¼ teaspoon nutmeg
1 orange, sliced in half moons

Preheat oven to 325°F. Put butter, brown sugar, orange juice, and lemon juice in a casserole or baking pan. Bake until butter has melted, about 5 minutes. Remove from oven.

Place bananas in casserole dish and sprinkle with cinnamon and nutmeg. Arrange oranges attractively around bananas or between the bananas. Bake 10 to 15 minutes, until tender. Serve warm or chilled.

Onion Casserole

Makes a 2-quart casserole

Super cook Auntie Lillian "Eio" Lee Chu made this dish for special occasions such as Thanksgiving. It is sweet from all the onions and creamy from the cheese and half-and-half.

3 cups water
2 teaspoons salt
½ cup uncooked rice
¼ cup unsalted butter
7 to 8 large onions, sliced

1 cup grated Swiss or Jarlsberg cheese
⅔ cup half-and-half or heavy cream
Salt and pepper to taste

Preheat oven to 325°F.

Bring water to a boil in a large pot. And salt. Add rice and cook 5 minutes. Drain and set aside.

In same pot, melt butter and sauté onions on medium-low heat until translucent, 10 to 15 minutes.

Add rice, cheese, half-and-half, salt, and pepper. Pour mixture into a 2-quart casserole and bake uncovered for 1 hour.

Easy Scalloped Potatoes

Serves 8 to 10

My mother's dear friend, Arlene Sullivan, shared this recipe with her. It reminds me of a good baked potato with sour cream and chives.

1 (30-ounce) package frozen hash brown potatoes, thawed
1 pint sour cream

1 (10.5-ounce) can condensed cream of mushroom soup
2 cups sharp cheddar cheese
1 cup chopped green onions or garlic chives

Preheat oven to 350°F. Mix all ingredients together in a large casserole and bake 1 hour uncovered. Serve hot.

Hold in Your Hand Guava Jell-O

Fills an 8 x 8-inch pan

This is a wonderful recipe to take to a soccer game. With the additional gelatin, the Jell-O stays firm enough that you can hold a piece in your hand.

2 cups water
⅔ cup sugar
1 (3-ounce) package strawberry-flavored Jell-O

1 (6-ounce) can frozen guava juice, defrosted
3 packages unflavored gelatin (such as Knox)
¾ cups water

Boil 2 cups water with sugar. Add Jell-O crystals and stir until dissolved. Add guava juice.

In a separate bowl, mix unflavored gelatin with ¾ cup water. Stir until it hardens. Mix in the Jell-O-juice mixture. Pour into an 8 x 8-inch pan and refrigerate until hard. Cut and serve.

Double recipe for a 9 x 13-inch pan.

Lime-Pineapple Jell-O Mold

Fills a 4-cup mold

Auntie Helen Noh Lee made this often. I always enjoyed the two-toned layers. The translucent green Jell-O contrasts with a white layer made of Jell-O mixed with cream cheese. I haven't been to a party with a Jell-O mold for at least twenty years. It's time for a Jell-O mold comeback.

1 (6-ounce) box lime-flavored Jell-O
1 (8-ounce) package cream cheese
1 (8-ounce) can crushed pineapple, juice reserved
Non-stick cooking oil spray
Optional garnish: Fresh berries or fruit

Prepare Jell-O according to package directions. Pour one quarter of the mixture in a large bowl and mix with cream cheese thoroughly. Mix in pineapple and pineapple juice. Set aside the remaining Jell-O and keep at room temperature.

Spray the inside of a 4-cup Jell-O mold. Add cream cheese-pineapple-Jell-O mixture to mold. Cover and refrigerate until hardened, about 1 hour.

Pour in the rest of the prepared Jell-O, cover and refrigerate overnight.

To unmold the Jell-O, dip the bottom of the mold in warm water to release the gelatin. Place a large plate or platter on the top of the mold and, holding the plate firmly, flip mold over. Refrigerate again until ready to serve.

Garnish with fresh or canned berries or fruit.

For larger molds, double the recipe.

Spicy Cranberry Relish

Makes 2½ cups

Auntie Lillian "Eio" Lee Chu made this relish for Thanksgiving. It is sweet, sour, and spicy, a refreshing change from the overly sweet sauces often served with turkey. Great with venison, duck, and other rich meats. Using a food processor simplifies this side dish, but the original chopping-by-hand procedure results in a better texture.

12 ounces fresh or frozen cranberries
1 clove garlic, minced
1 to 2 jalapeño chilies, minced (see note)
3 green onions, chopped

5 tablespoons finely chopped cilantro
⅓ cup fresh lime juice
½ cup sugar
Salt and pepper to taste

Boil cranberries in pot of water 1 minute. Drain. Squeeze or mash half the cranberries and leave the rest whole for a nice texture. Mix in garlic, chilies, green onions, cilantro, lime juice, and sugar. Taste and season with salt and pepper. Refrigerate until ready to serve.

Easy method: After boiling and draining the cranberries, put half in a blender or food processor with the garlic, chilies, green onions, cilantro, lime juice, and sugar. Blend until combined. Add the rest of the cranberries; taste and season with salt and pepper.

Note: Discard the seeds of the jalapeño if you want less heat.

Breads

For Asian American families in Hawai'i, the main starch was rice at each meal. My mother, though, often took a different tack, making a sweet cornbread for gatherings. She would add extra cornmeal to make it crunchy. See if you like her approach.

My mother wasn't above taking shortcuts. Our family was happy on weekends when my mother would make her Morning Biscuits. It is such an easy recipe using store-bought instant biscuits rolled in melted butter and coated with brown sugar and cinnamon. It's a perfect example of how convenience foods, combined with a little TLC, can create a family favorite.

Other top notch recipes include lavosh, the crispy flatbread, which was the rage in the 1970s. And you may enjoy the nice crumb of the Mango Loaf recipe. For special occasions, you may want to bake Sally Lunn rolls or the spoon rolls. They are the perfect vehicle for butter and some homemade guava jelly.

When you serve something fresh from the oven, your family will remember it forever.

Morning Biscuits with Cinnamon and Brown Sugar

Makes 8 biscuits

On weekends, my mother would serve this caramelized, warm biscuit for breakfast along with the preserved meat of the day—Spam, bologna, Portuguese sausage, Vienna sausage, luncheon meat, or corned beef hash. The combination of store-bought biscuits, butter, sugar, and cinnamon is an easy classic.

1 (16.3-ounce) can refrigerated biscuit dough (8 large)
½ cup butter, melted
¾ cup brown sugar

2 teaspoons ground cinnamon
Optional: ½ cup chopped walnuts, pecans or macadamia nuts

Preheat oven to 350°F. Unwrap and separate biscuits.

Place melted butter in one bowl; combine brown sugar with cinnamon in another bowl.

Line a 9 x 9-inch pan with foil. Dip biscuits in butter and coat thoroughly. Then cover with cinnamon sugar. Place in baking pan. If using nuts, sprinkle them on top. Bake 15 minutes, until nuts are toasted, sugar has turned to caramel, and biscuit is cooked through.

My siblings and I like to think that we ate quickly because, with five children at the table, we needed to eat fast to get our share. Brother Russell likes to joke that the rule at dinner was, "One foot on the floor at all times."

Variation: If you have a sweet tooth, cut the biscuits into fourths, double the amount of butter, sugar, and cinnamon and dip one by one.

Mango Loaf

Serves 10 to 12

Do you remember the days when everyone left mangoes outside your front door? Almost every house had a mango tree and people would scramble to find a use for the ripe fruit before it spoiled. Here is one recipe that takes advantage of the strong taste of mango. This loaf freezes well.

½ cup unflavored shortening, such as Crisco
1 cup sugar
2 eggs
1¾ cups flour
1 teaspoon salt
1 teaspoon baking powder
½ teaspoon baking soda
½ teaspoon cinnamon

½ teaspoon nutmeg
1 cup ripe mango, cut into ¼-inch cubes
½ cup chopped walnuts

Glaze:
½ cup powdered sugar
1 tablespoon water or milk

Preheat oven to 350°F. Line a 8½ × 4½ × 2½-inch loaf pan with parchment or foil.

In a standing mixer or large bowl, mix the shortening until soft. Add sugar, creaming until fluffy. Add eggs one by one until light and fluffy.

In a separate bowl, sift together flour, salt, baking powder, baking soda, cinnamon, and nutmeg. Add flour mixture to the shortening mixture in batches, alternating with mango cubes, beating after each addition. Stir in nuts. Pour into prepared pan and bake 1 hour, or until a pick inserted into center comes out clean.

Cool and remove loaf from pan. While loaf is still warm, mix powdered sugar with water or milk until blended; glaze cake. Serve warm or cool.

If freezing, you may want to glaze just before serving.

Grandma's Cornbread

Makes about 24 pieces

Many say this recipe should be called "corncake," as it is sweeter and lighter than most cornbreads that Southerners are accustomed to. Our family likes the crunch of a bit more cornmeal. The bread is a favorite with young and old, and our family calls it Grandma's Cornbread.

2 sticks butter, at room temperature
¾ cup sugar
2 eggs

1 cup whole milk
2 cups Bisquick baking mix
¼ teaspoon baking soda
¼ cup cornmeal

Preheat oven to 350°F.

In a standing mixer, cream butter and sugar. Add eggs and milk, then Bisquick, baking soda, and cornmeal. Mix 3 minutes. Pour into an ungreased 9 x 13-inch pan. Bake at 25 minutes (add 5 minutes if using a glass pan).

Insert a toothpick, skewer, or cake tester into center of the cake. If it comes out clean, the cornbread is done. Cool.

Cut into squares and serve or make honey butter (a 50:50 mix of butter and honey with a pinch of salt).

Variation: Coat 1½ cups fresh blueberries with 3 tablespoons of flour, then add in cornbread mixture just before baking.

Cooking should not cause stress. Just try recipes until you find one that you like. Keep making that dish until you have it memorized and can produce it easily ... It can become your signature dish.

Banana Bread

(based on the Old Kona Inn recipe)
Makes 3 (3 x 8-inch) loaves

It's funny that this banana bread is called the Old Kona Inn recipe. The Kona Inn in Kailua-Kona no longer serves this delicious bread— and who knows if it ever did. I find this recipe to have a strong banana taste, which I like. I've added nuts to the recipe, which I find really nice.

2 cups sugar	2 teaspoons baking soda
1 cup softened butter	1 teaspoon salt
3 cups mashed ripe bananas	1 cup chopped walnuts or pecans
4 eggs, well-beaten	Optional garnish: A few whole
2½ cups flour	nuts

Preheat oven to at 350°F. Grease and flour 3 loaf pans (3 x 8-inch).

In a large bowl, cream sugar and butter. Add bananas and eggs. Set aside.

In another bowl, sift together flour, baking soda, and salt. Mix with creamed mixture. Add nuts. Don't over mix. Pour into prepared pans. To make it fancier, add three whole walnuts or pecans on the top of each loaf as decoration.

Bake for about 1 hour. Test for doneness by inserting a wooden skewer in the middle of the loaf. If it comes out clean, it is done.

Cool and serve. Wrap leftovers in plastic wrap, then foil and freeze.

Note: You want your bananas so ripe that the skins are black. Freeze any leftover ripened bananas for a better flavor, and to use later.

Spoon Rolls

Makes about 24 rolls

Auntie Ethel Ching shared this recipe. It is a slightly sweet roll that is fantastic with butter and jam. What is better than home-baked dinner rolls for a holiday gatherings?

1 package (2¼ teaspoons) active dry yeast	¾ cup scalded milk
¼ cup lukewarm water	½ cup cold water
¼ cup sugar	1 egg
⅓ cup butter	3½ cups flour, sifted
1 teaspoon salt	Butter or oil to grease muffin tins

Dissolve yeast in lukewarm water in a small bowl. Set aside.

In a mixer, combine sugar, butter, and salt.

Cool milk by adding cold water, then add to batter in mixer. Blend in egg and the yeast mixture.

Add flour. Mix well until blended. It will be gummy. Place in greased bowl and cover; let sit in a warm, not windy, place, until double in size, about 45 to 60 minutes.

Punch down dough; spoon into well-greased regular-sized muffin tins, half full, or in a 9 x 12-inch pan. Let rise until dough rises to top, about 45 minutes.

Heat oven to 375°F. Bake 15 to 20 minutes. Serve warm or at room temperature.

Sally Lunn Dinner Rolls

Makes 24 Rolls

Auntie Ethel Ching taught me about this sweet bread said to have been invented in Bath, England. The rolls are sweet and soft like brioche.

1 cup hot whole milk
½ cup butter
¼ cup sugar
1 teaspoon salt
1 (¼-ounce) package dry active yeast

⅓ cup warm water
3 eggs
4 to 4½ cups flour
Butter to grease mixing bowl
Vegetable oil to grease baking sheets

In a large bowl, mix hot milk, butter, sugar, and salt. Let cool to lukewarm.

Stir yeast into warm water; let stand 5 minutes to dissolve.

Add yeast mixture and eggs to the milk mixture and beat vigorously. Gradually add flour. On a floured surface, knead dough for about 6 minutes until smooth and elastic. Form into a ball and place in a buttered bowl. Cover with a clean dish towel and let rise in a warm place until double in size, about an hour.

Preheat oven to 375°F. Lightly oil 2 baking sheets.

Punch down dough. Turn out onto a floured surface. Divide dough in half. Cover with a clean dish towel and let rest 10 minutes.

Divide each dough ball into 12 pieces. Gently shape each piece into a ball. Smooth tops by tucking in the edges. Place on prepared baking sheets. Cover with dish towel and let rise until nearly double, about 30 minutes.

Bake 10 to 12 minutes or until golden brown. Remove rolls from baking sheet and serve warm, or let cool on a rack.

Lavosh

Armenian Flat Bread

Serves 6 to 8

During a time in Hawai'i, this was considered a very high-class bread that was served at every country club. Now it is more commonplace, but still appreciated. It's a crispy flat bread that is broken in uneven shapes and enjoyed with butter or dips.

2¾ cups flour	½ cup butter at room temperature
¼ cup sugar	¾ cup buttermilk
½ teaspoon baking soda	Optional garnish: Poppy seeds
½ teaspoon salt	and sesame seeds to taste

Preheat oven to 400°F. Mix together flour, sugar, baking soda, and salt. With a knife, cut in butter until mixture has a fine crumb. Stir in buttermilk.

Roll dough into a ball and place on a floured cookie sheet with no sides. Sprinkle flour on rolling pin; roll dough flat. Sprinkle with sesame seeds and poppy seeds, if desired. Press seeds into dough. Bake until brown, about 4 minutes.

Note: Edges will brown faster than the center, so remove pan from oven, break off those edges and continue baking the center portion until done. Enjoy while crisp.

Desserts

When I was growing up, desserts were homemade. Very rarely would we see a store-bought pie, cake, or other sweet. At parties, specialties were proudly showcased. Auntie Ethel Ching's moist Classic Pound Cake was devoured, the crust and ends of her special huge Pullman loaves were fought over.

Many of the original dessert recipes in this chapter are a reflection of that time, when ingredients like "oleo-margarine" and Avoset were common in recipes. As much as I'd like to remain true to the originals, in many cases I've made revisions to take advantage of today's availability of fresh butter and whipping cream.

Enjoy the variety of these delectable desserts.

Apricot Mochi

Serves 20-plus

My mother would make this specially for her first grandchild, Sara Jean Grimes, who enjoyed it so much. The fruit flavor is very refreshing and different from the usual butter, coconut, or chocolate mochi desserts. The most difficult job is locating the apricot nectar.

Non-stick spray
1 (16-ounce) box mochiko (sweet rice flour)
2 (3-ounce) boxes or 1 (6-ounce) box apricot- or peach-flavored gelatin

2 cups sugar
1 (11.5-ounce) can apricot nectar
Potato starch

Preheat oven to 350°F. Coat a 9 x 13-inch baking pan with non-stick spray.

In a large bowl, mix rice flour, gelatin, sugar, and nectar with 1½ cans of water until thoroughly mixed. Pour mixture in pan and cover with foil. Bake 55 or 60 minutes, then remove pan from oven and let rest 15 minutes before removing foil. Cool at room temperature for several hours.

Cut with a plastic knife. Roll pieces in potato starch and serve.

Cookbook photographer Kaz Tanabe shares a Japanese cooking tip: After each cut into the sticky mochi, draw a metal knife through a piece of raw daikon. This works well to keep the knife clean and results in more precise mochi pieces.

Note: In many mochi recipes, potato starch and kinako (roasted soy bean flour) are used interchangeably to coat mochi desserts. Not here, though, as the kinako has a strong flavor that overpowers the subtle fruit flavor.

Coconut Butter Mochi

Makes 20 to 25 mini-florets or fills a 9 x 13-inch pan

The owners of Islands Marketing in Kalihi shared this recipe. Using the paper cups (florets) that they sell makes distributing this dessert easy. Using rice flour makes this a gluten-free treat.

1 (16-ounce) box (or 3½ cups) mochiko (sweet rice flour)
3 cups sugar
1 tablespoon baking powder
2 cups whole milk
½ cup (1 stick) butter, melted
5 eggs

1 teaspoon vanilla or coconut extract
1 (12 to 13.5-ounce) can coconut milk, thawed if frozen
1 cup grated coconut, sweetened or unsweetened

Preheat oven to 350°F. Place mini florets on a cookie sheet.

Mix all ingredients together. Pour batter into florets ¼-inch from top. Bake 25 to 35 minutes, until toothpick inserted in center of a floret comes out clean and the top is slightly browned. (These can be slightly over-baked, but don't under-bake.)

Note: This mochi can also be baked in a 9 x 13-inch cake pan, greased with butter or oil. Bake for 1 hour, or until a toothpick comes out clean. Also, substitute cupcake shells and place in muffin tins for the same individual-sized treats.

Double-Crusted Banana Pie

Serves 6 to 8

My father, Richard Lo, loved double-crusted banana pie from Violet's in Kalihi. The restaurant is no longer there, but the memory of this pie remains. This recipe attempts to recreate the Violet's famous dish.

2½ cups ripe bananas, cut into
   ¼-inch slices
1 cup pineapple juice
½ cup sugar
3 tablespoons flour
1 teaspoon cinnamon
1 teaspoon nutmeg

½ teaspoon salt
2 (9-inch) unbaked pie crusts (see
   page 119)
1 tablespoon butter
2 tablespoons whole milk
Optional: 2 tablespoons sugar

Preheat oven to 400°F. Soak sliced bananas in pineapple juice for 30 minutes. Drain juice.

In a large bowl, mix bananas with sugar, flour, cinnamon, nutmeg, and salt. Pour into 1 unbaked pie crust. Dot with butter. Use second pie crust to top pie; seal edges. Cut slits in crust. Brush with milk and sprinkle with sugar, if using. Bake 30 to 35 minutes, until golden brown. Cool before cutting.

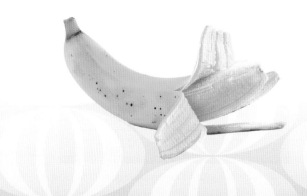

Blueberry Cream Cheese Pie

Makes 8 full slices

Of the many flavors of pie fillings, blueberry is Hawai'i's favorite. At every party I attend someone has made a version of this dessert. Change it up a bit with cherry, strawberry, lemon, or even apple fillings.

1 (9-inch) graham cracker pie crust (see recipe on page 120) or store-bought
1 (8-ounce) package cream cheese
¾ cup powdered sugar
1 tablespoon vanilla
1 cup heavy cream
1 (21-ounce) can blueberry pie filling

Preheat oven to 350°F. Line crust with foil and fill it with dried beans, raw rice, or pie weights, to keep the crust flat. Bake 15 to 20 minutes. Cool and set aside.

Using a stand or hand mixer, combine cream cheese, sugar, and vanilla until thoroughly mixed. Fold in heavy cream and pour into cooled pie crust. Refrigerate until firm, about 1 hour.

Top with blueberry filling. Serve immediately or refrigerate again.

Flaky Pie Crust and Custard Pie Filling

Makes 1 9-inch pie

The all-important crust recipe is modified from Auntie Adrienne Yee's recipe. Custard pie is such a favorite flavor in our state. It's not always offered in other locales.

Flaky Pie Crust:
1 tablespoon sugar
1 cup flour
1 teaspoon baking powder
¼ teaspoon salt
7 tablespoons Crisco shortening
3 tablespoons ice water
Flour for rolling out dough
1 egg white

Custard Filling:
4 eggs, plus 1 egg yolk, beaten
½ cup sugar
¼ teaspoon salt
½ teaspoon vanilla extract
¼ teaspoon nutmeg (grated is
   best)
2½ cups whole milk

For the crust: In a bowl, sift together sugar, flour, baking powder, and salt. In a standing mixer, mix shortening into flour mixture. Add water and mix until combined. Remove from mixer, form a ball, and wrap in plastic wrap. Chill at least 30 minutes.

Using lots of flour to cover work surface and rolling pin, roll out dough at least 1 inch larger than the 9-inch pie plate. Drape dough over pie plate, trim, and crimp edges. Cover with plastic wrap and chill at least 30 minutes.

Preheat oven to 400°F.

For the custard filling: Beat 4 whole eggs and the yolk in a large bowl. Add sugar, salt, vanilla, and nutmeg; mix. Set aside.

Heat milk in a pot over medium until hot, but not boiling. Pour ½ cup milk into egg mixture and stir until combined. Repeat slowly until all milk has been added. This gradual mixture avoids curdling the eggs.

Brush pie shell with egg white, including the edges. Fill crust and bake 30 to 35 minutes until center is set.

Cool at least an hour before cutting. Refrigerate leftover pie.

Lemon Ice Box Pie

Makes 1 (9-inch) pie

You know this is an old recipe when the refrigerator is called an ice box. This easy pie is similar to a key lime pie—sweet, yet wonderfully tart—and no baking is involved. Buying the crust already formed makes the pie even easier.

2 (14-ounce) cans sweetened condensed milk
½ cup fresh lemon juice (about 3 lemons)
Zest from 1 lemon
3 large egg yolks

1 (9-inch) store-bought graham cracker pie crust
2 cups heavy or whipping cream
¼ cup powdered sugar
Optional garnish: Thin slice of lemon for each piece

In a large bowl, whisk condensed milk with lemon juice and zest. Add egg yolks and mix 1 minute. Fill pie crust. Bake for 15 minutes at 375°F until crust is brown, but center is still jiggly. Cool. Refrigerate at least 2 hours or overnight.

Beat cream until it is whipped; add powdered sugar. Serve each piece of pie topped with a dollop of whipped cream and a slice of lemon.

From scratch way: Mix 1½ cups graham cracker crumbs with 6 tablespoons softened butter and press into a 9-inch pie pan. Bake 10 minutes at 350°F.

Fast way: Use defrosted Cool Whip instead of homemade whipped cream.

Pumpkin Chiffon Pie

Serves 8 to 12

A delicious holiday dessert from the Doan family of San Marino, California. Terry Doan Shelton was one of my college roommates and also lived in Hawai'i for a summer. She shared her mother Dudley's recipe with us.

1 tablespoon unflavored gelatin
  powder
1⅓ cups canned pumpkin
3 eggs, separated (see note)
¾ cup brown sugar
½ cup whole milk
2 teaspoons cinnamon
½ teaspoon salt
½ teaspoon ginger

½ teaspoon allspice
¼ teaspoon cream of tartar
6 tablespoons sugar
Garnish: Whipped cream

Crust:
1 cup butter, melted
1¼ cups finely crushed gingersnap
  cookies

Preheat oven to 325°F.

For the crust: In a bowl, mix butter and crushed ginger snaps. Press into a large pie plate and bake 7 to 8 minutes. Cool and set aside.

For the filling: Dissolve gelatin in ¼ cup cold water. Set aside.

In a saucepan, mix together pumpkin, egg yolks, brown sugar, milk, cinnamon, salt, ginger, and allspice. Heat while whisking continuously until mixture comes to a boil. Cook 1 minute, then remove from heat. Add dissolved gelatin and stir completely. Chill until partially set, then beat smooth with an electric mixer.

Beat egg whites with cream of tartar. When partially set, add sugar gradually, continuing to beat until stiff. Fold gently into pumpkin mixture. Pour filling into pie shell and let set in refrigerator 4 to 6 hours. Garnish with whipped cream.

Note: Since the egg white is not cooked, you may want to use pasteurized eggs.

New York-style Cheesecake

Serves 12 to 16

This makes a dense New York-style cheesecake, based on Eppie Lopez's recipe. Her daughter Melinda is a friend of mine from college days.

Crust:
18 graham crackers
¼ cup sugar
¼ cup melted butter

Filling:
3 (8-ounce) packages cream cheese at room temperature
4 eggs at room temperature
¾ cup sugar

Topping:
8 ounces sour cream
1 tablespoon vanilla extract
1 tablespoon sugar

Preheat oven to 350°F.

For the crust: Mix crackers and sugar in a food processor. Then mix in melted butter. Press into a 9-inch springform pan. Bake 15 minutes.

For the filling: Mix cream cheese, eggs, and sugar with a mixer until all lumps are gone.

Remove crust from oven and pour in filling. Increase oven temperature to 500°F. Bake 10 minutes more at that high heat, then turn down to 200°F and bake 1 hour longer.

Cool for at least 2 hours. May be served now without topping, or chill in refrigerator.

Combine topping ingredients. An hour before serving, spread topping on top of cheesecake and refrigerate. Serve by itself or with fresh berries mixed with a bit of powdered sugar.

"I Make Better" Pineapple Upside Down Cake

Serves 20

Before Sam Choy's Breakfast Lunch and Crab restaurant opened on Nimitz Highway, we were invited to preview samples of the food. The last dish was a pineapple upside-down cake. My mother took one bite and told the waiter, "Tell Sam Choy I make better." We still joke with my mother about her confidence—in fact, this cookbook should be called, "I Make Better," for her phrase. Here is her simple recipe for that dessert.

½ cup butter
1 cup packed brown sugar
1 (20-ounce) can pineapple slices, drained, but keep the juice
8 maraschino cherries, cut in half

1 (16.5-ounce) yellow cake mix, Duncan Hines preferred
⅓ cup vegetable oil
3 large eggs, at room temperature
½ cup water

Preheat oven to 350°F. Place butter in a 9 x 13-inch pan; melt butter in oven, about 5 minutes.

Sprinkle brown sugar over butter. Arrange pineapple slices in any pattern over sugar, cutting the slices so the entire pan is filled. Tuck cherries amid pineapple slices cut sides up.

Use a mixer to combine cake mix with oil, eggs, water, and ½ cup of the pineapple juice from the can. Beat 2 minutes. Pour batter over pineapples in cake pan. Bake 50 minutes, or until toothpick inserted in center comes out clean.

Let stand 5 minutes, then invert cake into a large serving plate, so pineapple layer is on top. Cool. Cut into 20 pieces.

Classic Pound Cake

Serves 20 plus

Auntie Ethel Ching would make this classic dessert for every family gathering. She was generous with me and gave me a Pullman baking pan so I could try to duplicate her winning cake. It freezes well and feeds a crowd. You may be more familiar with the pullman loaf for bread. It has four straight sides. It is named after the bread served in Pullman train cars. This recipe makes approximately 13 cups of batter. If you don't have a loaf pan that size, substitute three 5½ × 10½-inch loaf pans, or four 5 × 9-inch pans, and reduce the baking time.

1 pound butter, at room temperature
4 cups sugar
12 eggs, at room temperature

2 teaspoons vanilla extract
1 teaspoon salt
4 cups flour

Preheat oven to 350°F.

Using a mixer, mix butter and add sugar, 1 cup at a time. When thoroughly mixed, add eggs, 1 at a time. (Break eggs first in a separate bowl, just in case one is spoiled, and to keep shells out of the batter.)

Add vanilla and salt. Mix in flour, 1 cup at a time. Use a spatula to incorporate all ingredients thoroughly.

Line a Pullman pan with waxed paper or parchment. Bake 1½ hours, testing for doneness with a cake tester or bamboo skewer. Turn off oven and crack open door. Leave cake in oven as it cools, 30 to 60 minutes.

Remove from oven; cool thoroughly. Serve plain, dusted with powdered sugar, drizzled with a simple frosting of powdered sugar and milk, or with fresh berries.

Cake freezes well. Wrap with plastic wrap, then with foil. Thaw in refrigerator before cutting or frosting.

Variations:
- **Lemon:** Use lemon extract plus zest from 1 lemon in place of vanilla.
- **Almond:** Use almond extract instead of vanilla and add 1 (12.5-ounce) can almond cake and pastry filling (such as Solo brand). Often it is difficult to find the Solo brand in Hawaii so I buy it when I visit the mainland or order it online.
- **Orange:** Replace vanilla with orange extract and add orange zest.

Prune Cake

Makes 24 large pieces

Prune cake was so common when we were growing up. It was moist and appreciated. At weddings, it was wrapped to look like a pretty present called a groom's cake and given out as favors.

⅔ cup butter, at room temperature
1 cup sugar
4 eggs, at room temperature
1¼ cups whole milk
2½ cups flour
1¼ teaspoons baking powder
½ teaspoon salt
1½ teaspoons baking soda
1 teaspoon ground cinnamon
1 teaspoon ground nutmeg

1 cup dried and pitted prunes, chopped
Butter, oil or non-stick spray to grease the pan

Frosting:
1 cup butter, at room temperature
2 tablespoons heavy cream
1½ cups powdered sugar
1 teaspoon vanilla
1 cup pecans, chopped

Preheat oven to 350°F. Grease a 9 x 13-inch baking pan.

Use a mixer to beat the butter and sugar until fluffy. Add eggs one at a time. Gradually add milk.

In a separate bowl, sift together flour, baking powder, salt, baking soda, cinnamon, and nutmeg. Add to butter mixture in batches until incorporated. Add prunes. Pour into prepared pan. Bake 40 to 50 minutes, until a toothpick inserted into center comes out clean. Cool.

For the frosting: In a large bowl, mix butter, cream, powdered sugar, and vanilla until well-blended. Spread evenly over prune cake. Sprinkle with pecans.

Fresh Apple Cake

Makes a 9 x 9-inch cake, or approximately 12 regular-sized cupcakes

Every time I bake this cake, I am asked to share the recipe. The fresh apples make the cake very moist. What kind of apples should you use? My mother would tell you to buy whatever is on sale. All flavors of apples work.

¼ cup (½ stick) unsalted butter
¾ cup sugar
1 egg, beaten
1 cup flour
½ teaspoon baking soda
½ teaspoon cinnamon

½ teaspoon nutmeg
½ teaspoon salt
2 cups diced, unpeeled raw
   apples
Optional: Powdered sugar for
   topping

Preheat oven to 350°F. Line a 9-inch square pan with parchment.

Using a mixer, cream butter, then add sugar. Add in egg, then flour, and the remaining ingredients except the apples. Mix well. It will be thick.

Mix in apples. Place in baking pan. Bake 45 minutes, until a cake tester or toothpick comes out clean. Cool.

Cut cake and sprinkle with powdered sugar just before serving. Enjoy warm or at room temperature. It's even good if baked the day before. May also be topped with whipped cream and a slice of fresh apple or mint.

For cupcakes, bake in lined cupcake tin 25 to 30 minutes. For a 9 x 13-inch pan, triple the mixture and bake 1 hour and 20 minutes.

Tip: For the best "snowy" look, sprinkle cake with powdered sugar just before serving.

Sponge Cake

Serves 10 or more

Auntie Lillian "Eio" Lee Chu's second signature cake (look for her Lazy Daisy Cake on page 133) was this light classic. The citrus flavor makes it unforgettable.

8 eggs, separated	**½ teaspoon salt**
1 cup sugar	**1 teaspoon lemon extract**
1 cup cake flour	**2 tablespoons butter, melted**
⅓ cup orange juice, not concentrate	**Optional: 1 tablespoon lemon or orange zest**
½ teaspoon cream of tartar	**Oil or butter to coat the pan**

Preheat oven to 350°F. Grease a tube pan (also called angel food or chiffon cake pan).

Use a mixer to beat egg yolks with sugar until fluffy. Fold in flour alternately with orange juice.

In a separate bowl, beat egg whites with cream of tartar and salt until stiff. Fold into flour-yolk mixture. Add lemon extract, butter, and zest, if using. Pour into prepared pan and bake 35 to 40 minutes, until a cake tester or toothpick comes out clean.

Turn pan upside down and cool before unmolding cake.

Carrot Cake

Serves 20-plus

This is based on a recipe from my father's sister, Ethel Lo Ching, who was a terrific baker. This carrot cake is very moist.

3 cups finely grated raw carrots
4 eggs, separated
3 cups sugar
1½ cups vegetable oil
2 teaspoons vanilla
1 teaspoon salt
2 teaspoons cinnamon
1 teaspoon nutmeg

1 cup chopped walnuts
2 teaspoons baking soda
⅓ cup buttermilk

Frosting:
Juice of one orange
½ cup sugar
Optional: Zest of one orange

Preheat oven to 325°F. Grease and flour a tube pan or a 9 x 13-inch baking pan.

Use a mixer to combine carrots, egg yolks, sugar, oil, vanilla, salt, cinnamon, and nutmeg until mixed thoroughly. Add walnuts. Batter will be a very thick.

Combine baking soda with buttermilk. It will foam. Add to batter.

In a separate bowl, beat egg whites until stiff and fold into batter. Pour into prepared pan bake 1 to 1½ hours. Test for doneness and cool 15 to 20 minutes. Invert over a serving platter.

For frosting: In a saucepan, mix orange juice, sugar, and zest, if using, heat over low heat until sugar is dissolved. Pour over cake. Cut cake and serve.

Easy Poppy Seed Cake

Serves 20

This recipe was popular in the 1950s and '60s, when cake-making was made easy through the introduction of boxed mixes. My mother preferred the Duncan Hines brand over others.

2 tablespoons poppy seeds
1 cup hot water
Shortening or oil to grease pan
1 (16.5-ounce) box butter or
    yellow cake mix, Duncan Hines
    preferred

1 (3-ounce) box instant vanilla
    pudding mix
1 teaspoon almond extract
½ cup vegetable oil
4 eggs, beaten

Preheat oven to 350°F. Soak poppy seeds in hot water for at least 10 minutes. Grease pan with shortening or oil.

In a separate bowl, combine cake mix, pudding mix, almond extract, oil, and eggs. Add poppy seeds and water. Pour into the greased Bundt or chiffon cake pan. Bake for about 50 minutes, until a toothpick inserted into the middle of the cake comes out clean.

Let cool 10 minutes, then invert pan over a plate and unmold cake.

Icing is optional: Mix 1 cup powdered sugar mixed with 2 tablespoons whole milk and drizzle over cake.

Lazy Daisy Cake

Serves 12 to 20

This was a signature dish of my Aunt Lillian "Eio" Lee Chu. The broiling of the topping at the end makes it distinctive. Some bakers add coconut to the topping, but my family preferred it without.

Shortening, oil, or butter to grease the pan
1 cup whole milk
2 tablespoons butter, at room temperature
2 cups cake flour, or substitute all-purpose flour
1 teaspoon salt
3 teaspoons baking powder
2 cups sugar
4 eggs
1 teaspoon vanilla

Frosting:
6 tablespoons butter
⅔ cup brown sugar
4 tablespoons cream
1 teaspoon vanilla extract
1 cup chopped walnuts, pecans or macadamia

Preheat oven to 350°F. Grease a 9 X 13-inch cake pan with shortening or oil.

In a saucepan, scald milk, then add butter. Cool.

In a bowl, sift together flour, salt, and baking powder.

Use a mixer to beat milk and butter mixture with sugar, adding sugar gradually, until fluffy and lemon yellow in color.

In another bowl, beat eggs slightly and add vanilla.

Alternately, add egg mixture and flour mixture in batches to the milk-butter-sugar mixture. Pour into a greased 9 x 13-inch pan and bake for 30 minutes. Test for doneness by inserting a cake tester or toothpick.

For the frosting: Combine ingredients and spread over the warm cake. Broil at 450°F until warm and bubbly. Watch carefully. Cut into pieces and serve.

Butter Nut in a Cup Tartletts

Makes 2 dozen in mini cupcake pans

My aunt, Esther Lo Chinn, made these tasty, tiny bites of nuts. They are like mini pecan pies. She had a handy way of measuring the butter, cutting off an inch from a block, using most of it in the crust, and the rest in the filling.

Crust:
1 block butter, less 1 inch (6 tablespoons), at room temperature
3 ounces cream cheese, at room temperature
1 cup sifted flour

Filling:
½ cup sugar
1 egg
½ teaspoon vanilla
1 inch of the butter, leftover from making crust (2 tablespoons)
¼ cup chopped walnuts, pecans, or macadamia nuts
24 whole nuts, for garnish

Preheat oven to 350°F.

For the crust: Combine butter, cream cheese, and flour. Divide dough into 2 pieces. Divide each half into 12 balls, flatten each ball, and press into cupcake tins, forming a tiny bowl. Each half of dough should fill 12 mini cups. No need to line or grease the tins.

For the filling: Mix sugar, egg, vanilla, and butter. Divide chopped nuts among the crust bowls. Top with filling mixture. Top each cup with a whole or half nut. Bake 30 minutes. Serve warm or room temperature.

I am a believer in the joy of cooking. While others may decompress by gardening, exercising, or knitting, I relax by cooking. It is my art and I never worry about it being correct. Every dish is just one step away from being even better.

Caramel Cuts or Blondie Bars

Makes about 24 to 48 brownies

These chewy treats are called Caramel Cuts at Punahou School and Blondie Bars elsewhere.

1¼ cups packed brown sugar
1 cup sugar
½ teaspoon salt
1¼ sticks butter, melted

1½ teaspoons baking powder
2 cups all-purpose flour
3 large eggs

Heat oven to 375°F. Grease a 9 x 13-inch pan or line with parchment.

Use mixer to cream brown sugar, sugar, salt, butter, and baking powder. Add flour until thoroughly mixed in. Add eggs. Scrape down sides of bowl and mix on medium speed for 2 minutes. Press mixture evenly into pan. Bake 12 minutes on a lower rack.

Rotate pan. Bake another 13 to 18 minutes until top is golden brown. Brownies will rise gradually, then flatten. Turn off oven and leave brownies in for 5 minutes.

Remove from oven and cool on a rack 10 minutes. Cut while still warm with a serrated knife. If you wait until the brownies cool the tops will crack.

Waioli Tea Room Date Bars

Makes 9 to 16 pieces

Growing up in Mānoa Valley, we would pass the Salvation Army's Waioli Tea Room almost every day. It was famous for its delicious desserts. Here is one of the recipes that supposedly mirrors one of the popular offerings.

2 cups pitted dates
1 cup water
½ cup brown sugar
1 tablespoon flour
1 teaspoon vanilla

Crust:
2¼ cups quick-cooking rolled oats
1⅛ cups flour
1 cup brown sugar
1 teaspoon baking soda
1 cup butter, melted
Optional: Powdered sugar

Preheat oven to 350°F. Grease an 8 x 8-inch pan with butter or oil, or line with parchment.

In a saucepan over medium-low heat, cook dates, water, brown sugar, and flour until mixture is soft and thick, about 30 minutes. Add vanilla and set aside.

For the crust: In a bowl, mix oats, flour, brown sugar, baking soda, and butter. Press half of the crust into the bottom of prepared pan. Pour date filling over crust and spread evenly. Press remaining crust over the date layer.

Bake 20 to 25 minutes, until done. Cool, cut into pieces. Sprinkle with powdered sugar.

Krispy Krunch Kookies

Makes about 25 cookies

My mother made these cookies and we enjoyed the crispiness. The recipe is easily doubled.

½ cup butter, at room temperature
¾ cup sugar
1 egg, at room temperature
2 tablespoons whole milk

1 cup flour
¼ teaspoon baking soda
2 cups Rice Krispies or corn flakes

Preheat oven to 325°F.

Use a mixer to beat butter with sugar. Add egg and milk. Gradually add flour and baking soda. Fold in Rice Krispies or Corn Flakes. Drop batter by tablespoons 2 inches apart on cookie sheet. Cookies will spread. Bake 12 to 15 minutes.

Remove cookies from baking sheet immediately to cool on a rack. If left too long on the sheet, they will be too brittle and crack. Cool and enjoy.

Tip: Use an ice cream scoop to keep the cookies a uniform size.

Baked Apples

Serves 4

You rarely see Baked Apples on menus nowadays. Yet they are a solid dessert to serve cold or hot. Use your favorite variety of apple or whatever is on sale.

Juice of 4 lemons
4 large apples
½ cup raisins
½ cup brown sugar
Optional: ½ cup chopped walnuts
** or macadamia nuts**
2 cups apple juice

Glaze:
1 cup unsalted butter
½ teaspoon salt
2 cups brown sugar
2 teaspoons cinnamon

Preheat oven to 350°F.

Add lemon juice to 4 cups water and set aside.

Remove core of apples and peel the top third of each. Place apples in the lemon water to keep them from discoloring.

Mix raisins and sugar together, along with nuts, if using.

Remove apples from lemon water and fill cavity in centers with raisin-sugar mixture. Place in a deep baking pan. Add apple juice, cover with foil and bake 35 minutes.

For glaze: In a saucepan, melt butter with salt, brown sugar, and cinnamon. Set aside.

Remove from oven and test texture of apples. They should be soft. Remove foil and coat apples with glaze. Bake 5 more minutes.

Remove and cool. Serve immediately or refrigerate. Great with vanilla ice cream.

It's easy to forget that we didn't always have the abundance that we have access to now. My mother-in-law, Nobuyo Hirata Kanda, told me that when she was a child, she would visit a Moilili Christian church at Christmastime to receive a holiday present. She would marvel over a fresh red apple that was from Washington state. That was a special treat that the family would share.

Thai Tapioca Pudding

Serves 6 to 8

More recently, my mother has been fascinated with this easy and refreshing dessert. Bright mandarin oranges or purple sweet potatoes contrast with the white tapioca in coconut milk. To make it more elegant, refrigerate the pudding in individual cups or glasses.

7 cups water
1 cup small Thai tapioca beads
1 cup sugar
1 (12 to 13.5-ounce) can coconut milk

1 (11-ounce) can mandarin oranges, drained, or substitute
1 cup cooked Okinawan purple sweet potato, cut into ½-inch cubes

In a pot, bring water to a boil. Add tapioca and cook about 30 minutes over medium-high heat until pearls are glassy.

Add sugar and stir until dissolved. Remove from heat. Cool for 10 minutes.

Add coconut milk. Chill until thickened, at least an hour and preferably overnight.

Before serving, add mandarin oranges or cooked sweet potato pieces.

Note: If you can't find small tapioca beads, use 1¼ cups medium-sized pearls with 10 cups water and 1¼ cups sugar.

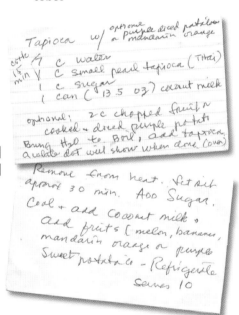

Glossary

Aburage: deep-fried tofu pockets

'Ahi: Hawaiian name for yellowfin tuna

Aku: Hawaiian name for skipjack tuna

Araimo: Japanese taro

Chuba iriko: dried anchovies

Daikon: Japanese white radish

Dashi: Japanese word for clear, light, basic fish broth. Sold as instant stock in granules, tea bags, or as a concentrate.

Gobo: Japanese word for burdock root

Hasu: Japanese word for lotus root

Hawaiian chili pepper: a very small and extremely hot chili pepper grown in Hawai'i

Hawaiian salt: White, coarse sea salt

Hijiki: Japanese word for a brown sea vegetable

Hokkigai: Japanese name for the Arctic Surf Clam

Japanese cucumber: smaller and thinner skinned than most cucumbers

Japanese eggplant: purple or green smooth-skinned fruit; long and thin, as opposed to the round eggplant

Kamaboko: Japanese word for red and white fish cakes made of puréed white fish mixed with potato starch and salt, then steamed

Kim chee base: spicy sauce base for the Korean pickled vegetable dish

Kitchen Bouquet: browning and seasoning sauce

Konbu: Japanese word for dried kelp (seaweed)

Konnyaku: Japanese word for a gelatinous cake made from the starch of a tuber called devil's tongue or konjac.

Liquid smoke: water-soluble liquid used for adding a wood smoke flavor to food

Mirin: sweet Japanese rice wine

Mochiko: flour made from mochi rice

Nishime konbu: Japanese word for thin kelp

Ocean salad: a salad generally consisting of wakame, seaweed ribs, sesame seeds, sesame oil, rice vinegar, sugar, and salt

Ogo: Japanese word for a reddish-brown seaweed; called limu in Hawaiian

Rice vinegar: a relatively mild vinegar

Shiitake mushroom: woodsy, smoky flavor mushroom; can be found dried or fresh

Shiofuki konbu: salted dried kelp strips

Shirataki: Japanese word for gelatinous, noodle-like strips made from tuberous root flour

Soba: Japanese buckwheat noodles

Takuan: Japanese pickled radish, often dyed bright yellow

Togarashi shichimi: Japanese seven-flavored spice; blend of pepper leaf, poppy seed, rape seed, hemp seed, dried tangerine peel, and sesame seed

Twist peppers: Korean pepper similar to the Japanese shishito pepper

Wakame: Japanese word for dried seaweed

Warabi: fiddlehead fern shoots; called hō'i'o in Hawaiian

Water chestnuts: popular ingredient in Chinese cuisine, known for its crunchy texture

Index

About the Author

Lynette Lo Tom relaxes by cooking. She is always ready for a food adventure and believes in continuous learning.

She is the author of *A Chinese Kitchen*, part of the *Hawai'i Cooks* series of cookbooks that highlights the ethnic diversity that is our state.

Lynette is a freelance food writer and regular contributor to the *Honolulu Star-Advertiser's* Crave food section. Her columns are "Back in the Day" and "Easy-Kine Cooking."

Before she started writing about food, she was a journalist at many different media. She was a marketing and public relations consultant for 25 years with her company, Bright Light Marketing. Contact her at lynette@brightlightcookery.com

Her favorite color is red and her cravings for food change daily.

Also by the author

ISBN: 978-1939487-52-0
Hardcover, wire-o
6 x 9 in. • 216 pp